GIANTS OF ART AND CULTURE

Pablo Picasso

Greatest Artist of the 20th Century

Pablo Picasso

Greatest Artist of the 20th Century

by
Patricia A. MacDonald

BLACKBIRCH PRESS, INC.

WOODBRIDGE, CONNECTICUT

Published by Blackbirch Press, Inc.
260 Amity Road
Woodbridge, CT 06525
Web site: http://www.blackbirch.com
e-mail: staff@blackbirch.com
© 2001 Blackbirch Press, Inc.

First published as *Pablo Picasso Genius! The Artist and the Process* by Silver Burdett Press, Inc., a division of Simon & Schuster, Inc., Prentice Hall Bldg., Englewood Cliffs, NJ, 1990.

Printed in the United States

10 9 8 7 6 5 4 3 2 1

Library of Congress Cataloging-in-Publication Data
MacDonald, Patricia A.
    Pablo Picasso : greatest artist of the 20th century / by Patricia A. MacDonald.
        p. cm.—(Giants of art and culture)
    Originally published: Englewood Cliffs, NJ : Silver Burdett Press, 1990.
    Includes index.
    ISBN 1-56711-504-7 (alk. paper)
    1. Picasso, Pablo, 1881–1973—Juvenile literature. 2. Artists—France—
Biography—Juvenile literature. [1. Picasso, Pablo, 1881–1973. 2. Artists. 3. Painting,
French. 4. Painting, Modern—20th century—France. 5. Art appreciation.] I. Picasso,
Pablo, 1881–1973. II. Title. III. Series.
N6853.P5 M3 2001   00-053003
709'.2
[B]

(Frontispiece)
Picasso in a whimsical mood at Vallauris. The rolls were made at a local bakery and known as "Picasso's Hands."

Contents

Chapter 1	Childhood and Youth	7
Chapter 2	In Barcelona	21
Chapter 3	Experiments in Art and Life	29
Chapter 4	Cubism	45
Chapter 5	Years of Growth and Conflict	59
Chapter 6	The War Years	73
Chapter 7	A Place in the Sun	85
Chapter 8	"Nothing Is More Important..."	101
Chapter 9	Retrospective	111
Chronology		114
Glossary		120
Bibliography		123
Index		125

A picture lives its own life,
like a living creature.

—Pablo Picasso

CHAPTER 1

CHILDHOOD AND YOUTH

Pablo Ruiz Picasso was born in Málaga, Spain, in 1884. It was a time of great changes in the world—a time very much like our own. People everywhere, especially young people, were excited about new ideas and new ways of doing things. Faster ships, rail travel, the telegraph, and other inventions had brought different parts of the world closer together in the years before Picasso's birth. People who had been long oppressed, like peasants and factory workers, were uniting to demand a better way of life from their governments. The need for personal freedom was more widely felt and expressed. And people were willing to struggle for it.

As so often happens, the artists of the day were among the first to sense the spirit of the times. They expressed it in new kinds of painting, sculpture, poetry, music, and other forms of creativity. But these works were often unpopular at first, simply because they were so different from what people were used to.

It was from this background of rapid growth and change that the young Picasso would move into leadership of the movement that we now call modern art. It was, in fact, a whole new way of seeing things in the light of the troubled twentieth century—a mirror held up to human life as we know it. Years later Picasso would tell a friend: "I have never painted anything but my time."

A king, Alfonso XII, ruled Spain from Madrid, the capital city. His powers were limited by a constitution. The real power was held by the wealthy landowners, who formed a very small part of the population. Most of the Spanish people lived in poverty.

Picasso's father, Don José Ruiz Blasco, came from a well-respected family long established in the province (state) of Andalusia. The Ruiz family had lived in the southern seaport of Málaga for more than a hundred years, and they were known as people of good taste and manners. But they were by no means wealthy. Every member of the family had to earn his own livelihood, rather than living on inherited money or income from land. Don José's surname, Blasco, was that of his mother. (Most Spaniards use the last names of both their parents, but Pablo Picasso was an exception. In his early twenties he dropped the surname of Ruiz and used only his mother's name when he signed his work. Ruiz is a very common name in Spain, and the young artist and his friends felt that Picasso was more memorable.)

Picasso's father Don José Ruiz Blasco in 1870, a melancholy artist, a teacher, and the major influence in Picasso's early artistic life.

As a young man, Don José showed such promise as an artist that his older brother Pablo, a clergyman with no family of his own, became his patron. It was not easy, then or now, to gain recognition and earn a living as an artist. Thus men and women of means have often helped to support young painters, musicians, and others who would have been unable to exercise their talents without financial aid. A patron also serves to make an artist's work better known and may introduce him to art dealers and others who will help find a market for the artist's paintings.

Don José worked hard, but his pictures did not always sell. When they did, it was mainly to people who wanted something to decorate their dining rooms. As a result, his work consisted largely of "still lifes"—pictures of flowers, fruit, and other nonliving things. They were pretty but uninspired. In them, the viewer saw exactly what he (and everyone else) expected to see.

Finally, Don José's ten brothers and sisters got together and decided that he had to start supporting himself. It was all very well to dream of being an artist, they declared, but it was time he married and settled down. In fact, they had already picked his future wife, as was the custom. But in this matter, gentle Don José showed unusual spirit. He had already chosen a wife for himself—the dark-eyed, lively, and outgoing Maria Picasso Lopez. And to make matters even more embarrassing for his family, she was a cousin of the girl they had chosen for him!

However, the two young people were in love, and there was nothing the family could do but agree to their marriage. Physically, they were very unlike. Don José was tall, slender, and fair-haired, while Doña Maria was small and vivacious, with lustrous black hair and intense dark eyes. But emotionally they were well matched. His fiancée's good humor and eagerness for life offset Don José's natural shyness, and the affection between them was deep and lasting. They were married in 1880 and took an apartment in a tall whitewashed building on Málaga's Plaza de la Merced (Market Square). Here Picasso would spend his early years.

In Spain and many Hispanic countries, the plaza is the traditional gathering place for everyone who lives in the city or town. Children play in the shade of its trees while their mothers talk with friends and keep a careful eye on them. In the evening, groups of girls of marriageable age stroll around the plaza laughing and pretending to be unaware of the young men who gather to talk and watch them admiringly. On special feast days (*fiestas*), colorful religious processions depart from the churches and cathedrals to wind their way through the streets. Their ranks are continually increased by onlookers who join in to pray or throw flowers in the path of the images of saints that are carried in the procession. All around the plaza, benches and open-air cafes provide a place to relax in an unhurried atmosphere while watching the world go by.

Málaga's location on the Mediterranean Sea gives it a warm, sunny climate that has made it a popular resort area as well as a busy port. In the late nineteenth century, many people traveled there for holidays. The air was fragrant with the sea breezes and the odor of fruits and flowers. Oranges and lemons were grown nearby for the market, and fine wines were made from the local grapes.

On holidays, the people of Málaga dressed in gaily colored traditional costumes like those of the Andalusian Gypsies who originated the rhythmic *flamenco* style of song and dance. Ruffled skirts whirled and booted heels tapped out the rapid rhythm of the dance. At Málaga's huge outdoor arena, thousands of fans gathered for the traditional bullfight, which would play such an important part in Picasso's art. First, the *picadores* would enter the ring on horseback and anger the bull by pricking it with lances. Then the *banderilleros*, on foot, would thrust a pair of darts into the animal. Finally, the *matador* entered the ring on foot, with cape and sword, and engaged the bull in a series of charges and retreats. Usually, the unequal contest ended in the bull's death; sometimes, in the

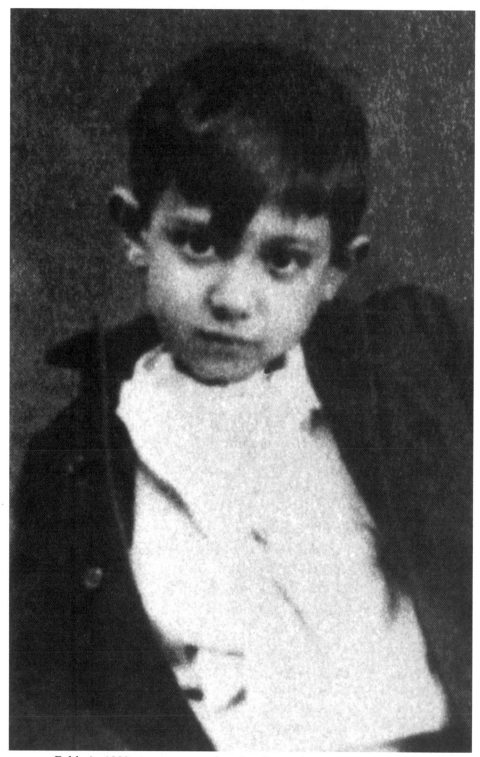

Pablo in 1888 at age seven, already a keen observer.

matador's. Occasionally, a brave bull's life would be spared at the demand of the crowd.

This blood sport originated in Roman times and recalled the Greek myth of the Minotaur—a monster with the body of a man and the head of a bull, who was confined in the great Labyrinth on the island of Crete until it was killed by the hero Theseus. The Roman emperors imported the fierce wild bulls of Spain for their contests in the arena, and the Moors of North Africa developed the bullfight into a highly stylized performance, a kind of ritual dance between man and beast.

After the Moorish conquest of Spain, around A.D. 700, the bullfight became so much a part of Spanish culture that no effort to ban the practice was successful. No matter how many *matadors* died in the ring, or how many animals suffered, the spectacle continued, and still does. In Hispanic cultures, it is not considered cruelty. As the American writer Gertrude Stein, a friend of Picasso's, explained: "To a Spaniard, it is not bloodshed, it is ritual." And few cultures have a deeper reverence for ritual and tradition than the Spanish.

A year after the marriage of Don José and Doña Maria, their first child, a sturdy dark-haired boy, was born on October 25, 1881. A few days later, the young couple brought the baby to their parish church for baptism.

In the Roman Catholic faith, it is customary to baptize a child with the name of a saint, who will be the child's spiritual patron throughout life. The practice in Málaga was to give a child as many saints' names as possible, some of which were also the names of his ancestors. And some of these saints had long honorary titles as well, such as Cyprian of the Most Holy Trinity, or Our Lady of Help, for the Virgin

Mary. All these heavenly and earthly patrons were invoked at the baptism of young Pablo. His full Christian name—believe it or not—was Pablo Diego José Francisco de Paula Juan Nepomuceno Maria de los Remedios Cipriano de la Santissima Trinidad. Fortunately, only one of these names was actually used. The name Pablo (the Spanish form of Paul) was given in honor of the uncle who had supported his father's work and had died shortly before his nephew's birth.

The first sights and sounds of Picasso's life were in a rambling apartment building on Market Square. The poets, painters, and musicians of Málaga gathered around the square, and its atmosphere was appealing to Don José, who had many friends with creative interests. After his son's birth, Don José took a teaching job with the School of Fine Arts and Crafts so that he could support his family. From that time on he would always be a teacher of art. But he continued working at his own paintings, too. In fact, when money was scarce, the landlord sometimes agreed to take a painting instead of the rent. Don José was a popular figure whose friends called him "the Englishman" because of his distinguished appearance, fair coloring, and formal manners.

Pablo was fortunate in having a family that could recognize early signs of artistic talent. Later, his mother would say proudly that the child's first word was an urgent "'piz, 'piz!"—for lápiz, meaning pencil. Imitating his father, he covered sheet after sheet of paper with spirals, lines, and later, simple forms. In fact, he could draw before he could talk. And his striking black eyes looked deeply into everything around him.

Within a few years, Pablo would amuse his sisters and cousins by drawing all kinds of animals on demand. It was a game, in which he put pencil to paper and awaited instructions. "A rabbit!" someone cried excitedly. And he would sketch, with incredible speed, a pair of ears, head and back, tail and feet— whatever was suggested as the starting point. Each line flowed effortlessly into the other until the picture was complete. Someone else would demand an ele- phant, beginning with the ear. And the animal ap- peared as if by magic.

However, like many child prodigies, Pablo could also be very hard to live with. He was a self-centered child who would remain self-centered all his life. Quick to make fun of others, he could never bear to be mocked himself, and his temper was sometimes vio- lent. From an early age, he made it clear that his work came before everything else in his life: family, social life, religion, relationships of every kind. And those who loved him most were the likeliest to suffer his criticisms, rages, and resentments.

Don José encouraged his son to ask questions and to watch all that he did in his studio. He himself was always trying out new techniques. If he was working on a large picture of pigeons—his favorite subject—he would draw many birds, at rest or in flight, then cut them out and rearrange them until he was satisfied with his composition. Only then did he begin the full- scale painting. This was a form of the cut-paper, or collage, style in Spanish art, which would be very prominent in Picasso's work. It was, perhaps, the source of Pablo's lifelong practice of making dozens of preliminary sketches and studies in his notebooks before starting a major painting or sculpture.

Painting and pigeons were two passions that Picasso shared with his father. Like many Spaniards, they kept these gentle birds, which are members of the dove family, as pets. The many shades of color in their feathers, ranging from soft blue-gray to tones of

A study of six pigeons and a bullfight, from Pablo's early sketch-book.

buff and ivory to the shimmering green of a peacock's tail, could well inspire an artist. Pigeons are such a common sight that we may not notice the uniqueness of each individual bird. Of a hundred birds in a city park, no two are identical in their markings. These sociable animals are very much at home with people, looking eagerly for crumbs from those who enjoy feeding them. It is amusing to watch their slow, high-stepping walk and their short bursts of flight when something startles them. It is an artist's business to to notice such things and record them for the rest of us so that we may see them with a fresh eye.

Picasso's earliest memory that was outside the calm and happiness of his family life was of the great earthquake that struck Málaga when he was three years old. Years later, he described that day to his friend Jaimé Sabartés. The ground under the city was shaking, and chunks of masonry fell from the buildings. His father rushed into the apartment, which was on the second floor, to take them to a safer place at ground level. His wife was about to give birth to their second child, and they were all very frightened.

"My mother wore a handkerchief on her head," recalled Picasso. "I had never seen her like that before. My father seized his cape from the coat stand, threw it round his shoulders, took me in his arms and rolled me in its folds." They had scarcely reached the safety of a friend's house near the harbor when Doña Maria went into labor. That night, Picasso's sister Lola was born.

The earthquake had not destroyed their home at 36 Market Square, and the family returned there to everyday life. The new baby was a source of great happiness, and she and her brother soon formed a close relationship that would last a lifetime. Dark-haired, Lola looked very much like her mother and brother, and she became one of Picasso's favorite subjects. He made many sketches of her and other family members, as he was almost never without a pencil in his hand from the time he was seven years old. He also drew the people whom he saw in the plaza and the city streets, the children of friends, and imaginary scenes of his own creation. Both his parents continued to encourage his talent and saved many of his drawings, including *El Picador*, his first bullfight scene.

Except for art, however, young Pablo hated school. He could scarcely be persuaded to go unless he was allowed to take a pet pigeon with him. And then he spent all his time drawing pictures of it, instead of learning the alphabet! His teachers didn't know what to do with him. It was clear that he was very intelligent, but he was totally absorbed in his art.

In 1888 Picasso's sister Concepción was born. His parents were happy to have another daughter, but now Don José had to struggle hard to make ends meet for his growing family. As their poverty increased, he felt more and more discouraged. Finally, against his own wishes, he decided to accept a better-paying teaching job at the Instituto da Guarda, a high school in La Coruña, far from his relatives and friends. The family moved there in 1891.

La Coruña was very different from Málaga. Located on Spain's rough, rocky Atlantic coast, it had a wet, chilly climate that Don José disliked at once. The long, gray days depressed him, and he missed the warm friendships and the close family ties of his native city. Only Pablo, now ten years old, seemed enthusiastic about his new surroundings. He joked about the weather and sent his relatives in Málaga pictures of people whose umbrellas were being blown inside out by the wind. As always, he was deeply interested in everything around him.

The family had been in La Coruña only a few months when they suffered a great loss. Three-year-old Concepción, a pretty, blonde child who resembled her father, caught the dreaded disease of diphtheria and died. There was no vaccine against this highly contagious disease in those days, and some families lost more than one child during the severe epidemics that broke out. High fever and difficult breathing were the symptoms, and stricken parents watched helplessly as the disease took its course.

The family had taken an apartment very close to the school where Don José taught, and perhaps his son's growing skill as an artist was some comfort for the loss of the daughter who had looked so much like her father. Pablo spent much of his time at the school, learning to draw in charcoal and making excellent copies of the classical statues that the older students used as models. (At this time, few students drew "from life"—that is, from a living model.) But despite his son's talent, Don José still worried about his total lack of interest in his other studies. Finally, he enlisted the help of a kindly teacher who was willing to engage the boy's attention by way of his favorite subject.

Asked what he knew about math, Pablo assured the teacher—quite truthfully—that he knew nothing, "strictly nothing." Then the teacher drew a column of numbers on the blackboard and asked the boy to try and add them up. The problem was a complete mystery to Pablo—until he began to see it as a drawing. Then, he would recall, inspiration struck. "The eye of the pigeon is round like zero. Under the zero a six, with a three under that. There are two eyes and two wings. The two legs placed on the table underline it, and below that there is the total!" He would never be a mathematician, but at least he would finish school. His parents sighed with relief.

The family lived in La Coruña for four years until Don José was offered a job at the school of Fine Arts in Barcelona (La Lonja). This position as an instructor of drawing and painting was a step up in his career, and Barcelona was a sophisticated city, unlike the provincial port of La Coruña. It was the center of intellectual life in Catalonia—a province that had always prided itself on its independent spirit because of its location in northeastern Spain. And the Catalans considered themselves more international in their outlook than other Spanish people. Beyond the Pyrenees—the mountain range between northern Spain and France—they saw a wider world.

Pastel of Picasso's mother (1895), drawn shortly after he and his family moved to Barcelona.

CHAPTER 2

IN
BARCELONA

Happy to leave La Coruña behind him, Don José took his wife and children to Málaga for a summer reunion. He joined the staff of La Lonja in the fall of 1895. The following year, the fifteen-year-old Pablo was admitted to the art school where his father taught. His performance on the entrance examination astonished the faculty: he completed in one day the demanding figure study for which a full month was allowed. So rapid was the boy's development that two years before, his father had given up painting altogether and handed over all his paints and brushes to his son in recognition of his greater gifts.

Now that Don José's fortunes had improved, he rented a studio for Pablo in the Calle de la Plata (Silver

Street). Here, the young artist produced many striking portraits of his family and friends. His sister Lola remained one of his favorite subjects. By now, she was growing into a beautiful young woman. He also painted his elderly Aunt Pepa and his Uncle Salvador, the doctor who had assisted at his birth. It was difficult to believe that these striking likenesses, including the remarkable *Portrait of the Artist's Mother*, were the work of a teenage boy. In this portrait, Doña Maria is seen in profile with her head slightly bowed. The slenderness of youth has given way to the solidity of middle age, and the many difficulties of her life, as well as its joys, are conveyed by line, color, and the profound feeling imbued by the artist. Picasso showed true self-knowledge when he said of his art, "I want the work to reflect only feeling."

It was also in his first studio that Picasso painted the symbolic picture entitled *Science and Charity*—the first work that he exhibited to the public. His father served as the model for the doctor at a patient's bedside, who represented Science. A nun holding a newborn child symbolized Charity; there were several nuns in his family who could have served as models. This work was awarded Honorable Mention in an art show in Madrid in 1897.

That same year Picasso's Uncle Salvador recommended that he continue his studies at the Royal Academy of San Fernando in Madrid—the major art school in Spain at this time. Again, Picasso passed the entrance examinations with ease, but the teaching at the academy was too rigid and formal for his taste. He soon tired of copying plaster models and grew homesick for Barcelona, where the atmosphere was more stimulating. But one thing he did like about Madrid was the Prado, Spain's National Museum of Painting and Sculpture. In this treasure house of Spanish art, he could study the work of such masters as El Greco (the Greek, Doménikos Theotokópoulos), who was born on the island of Crete about 1541 but settled in Toledo, Spain, in his mid-thirties. He died there in 1614.

El Greco's powerful paintings conveyed the mysticism—deep religious experience—of his adopted country by way of long, thin figures that appeared to be reaching from earth toward heaven. Their upturned eyes seemed to look into another world. In his masterpiece *The Burial of Count Orgaz*, El Greco broke through to a new vision of the relationship between the natural and the supernatural. Picasso and his friends "rediscovered" El Greco in the late 1800s, and his influence is unmistakable in certain of Picasso's pictures like *The Burial of Casagemas*.

Another Spanish artist who affected Picasso strongly was Diego Velázquez (1599-1660), who was appointed court painter to King Philip IV in 1623. His penetrating character studies of the Spanish royal family, painted over a period of thirty-seven years, made him the greatest painter of his day and one of the most gifted portrait painters in history. The Prado's collection included fifty paintings by Velázquez, among them *The Surrender of Breda*, *The Spinners*, and *Las Meninas* (*The Maids of Honor*), his masterpiece. This enormous painting included a representation of the artist himself, with brush and palette, working on a large canvas—a theme that would echo through Picasso's work throughout his career. The painter is gazing at a mirror in which the king and queen are reflected. Like Velázquez, Picasso was fascinated by the creative process itself. Late in his life he would paint a whole series of pictures "after Velázquez"—that is, reinterpreting *Las Meninas* in the terms of modern art.

At the National Museum, Picasso also studied the work of Francisco de Goya (1746-1828). Goya's passionate depiction of the horrors of war in such paintings as *The Third of May, 1808* (when Spanish citizens were massacred by French soldiers under Napoleon) foreshadowed Picasso's masterpiece *Guernica*, which depicted the horrors of the Spanish Civil War. Goya was also a court painter, to King Charles IV. Like Velasquez, he made a portrait of the entire royal family that included himself in the act of painting. This work and others contributed to Goya's reputation as the greatest painter to bridge the eighteenth and nineteenth centuries. Like El Greco before him, Goya's innovative work made him a forerunner of contemporary art.

Late in 1897, Picasso contracted scarlet fever, which left him weak and depressed. Now eighteen years old, he left Madrid to spend the early part of 1898 in the country with his friend Mañuel Pallarés. In the small village of Horta de Ebro, the city-bred Picasso discovered in himself a love for the rugged outdoor life of the Spanish peasant. He swam in the cold streams of the province of Aragon, ate plain but wholesome foods, and recovered his health. At the same time, he became familiar with the simple work of the local craftsmen, who knew nothing of the pretentious art of the Royal Academy. "The academic gospel of beauty," he declared, "is a fraud."

Like the people of Horta de Ebro, Picasso saw what was real (natural) in the world around him— both the beautiful and the brutal—and re-created it in his work. So lasting was the impression of this visit that he would say later, "Everything I know I learned in the village of Pallarés."

As Hans Jaffé pointed out in his excellent study of Picasso, "His curiosity, his sensibility, were so univer-

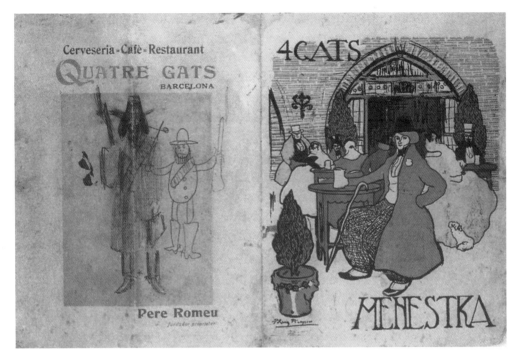

Menu cover from Els Quatre Gats, a regular meeting place for artists and intellectuals in Barcelona.

sal that they could not be confined to a single area of painting, nor even to painting alone. Picasso was one of the few universal artists of our time—and it was his authenticity that made him universal."

From this point on, the young artist moved away from the familiar models he had used since childhood. After his return to Barcelona, he drew and painted increasingly from memory, or found his subjects on the streets of the Spanish city, as he would later in Paris. He was encouraged to try new paths by the circle of young artists and intellectuals who met regularly at the Barcelona cabaret called Els Quatre Gats (The Four Cats). They were excited about the currents of thought flowing from Germany, England, and France. They might debate all night about the merits of French Impressionist painting and Art Nouveau (New Art), as seen in the work of England's Aubrey Beardsley and France's Henri de Toulouse-Lautrec. Politically, the young modernists favored sweeping changes in government and society that would lead to greater personal and artistic freedom. In fact, many of the Catalan intellectuals were anarchists—those who believe in no government at all.

In this circle, Picasso made many friends, including the painter Carlos Casagemas and Jaimé Sabartés, who wanted to be an artist but could not because a serious eye infection in childhood had left him half-blind. Sabartés was a gloomy young man who saw the negative side of everything. He had a long, thin nose and thick-lensed glasses, through which he squinted anxiously at the world. Sabartés admired Picasso's work deeply and developed a strong loyalty to him.

Later in life, Sabartés worked as Picasso's secretary for twenty-five years, jealously guarding him from the many hangers-on who gathered at the studio to admire his work (and to waste his time, as Sabartés saw it). Françoise Gilot, a young French painter who was Picasso's common-law wife for eight years after World War II, described Sabartés with humor in her book *Life with Picasso*:

> When people arrived at the *atelier* [studio] and met Sabartés, peering out through his thick glasses, completely absorbed in his own melancholy, and from time to time sadly dropping a word or two that eventually might add up to a whole sentence, that was enough to damp down the most buoyant enthusiasm. Most people under his scrutiny began to feel very guilty and stumble over their words. As a rule, the mere sight of his mournful, almost tragic expression and manner could get rid of the more timid visitors.

Another friend whom Picasso met in Barcelona was the painter and art historian Miguel Utrillo, who encouraged the young artists of the Catalan circle. It was Utrillo who would review Picasso's first one-man show with high praise in the art magazine *Pel y Ploma* (*Fur and Feather*, for brush and quill, tools of the artist and the writer). "He draws because he sees," said Utrillo admiringly, "and not because he can do a nose from memory."

In the year 1900, the nineteen-year-old Picasso was ready to make his first visit to Paris—the cultural capital of the Western world. Packing canvas and brushes, he crossed the Pyrenees with his friend Casagemas and discovered the city that would become his home for almost half a century.

Picasso in his Paris studio on Rue Schoelcher. He is standing
before his painting *Man Leaning on Table* (1916).

CHAPTER 3

EXPERIMENTS IN ART AND LIFE

It was not at all surprising that Picasso should be captivated by the city of Paris at first sight. Its spacious boulevards and parks, museums and monuments filled with art treasures, crumbling tenements side by side with elegant townhouses, bustling outdoor markets and cafes, rich and varied cultural life—all this could only be spellbinding. Young artists, writers, musicians, actors, and dancers flocked to the city's gates at the turn of the century, as they had for the previous 300 years. The great city on the banks of the Seine drew aspiring artists, collectors of art, students, and intellectuals with an irresistible attraction. As Russell Page wrote, "Paris is in itself a work of art—and greater, in this respect, than any of its individual buildings. It so happens that Notre-Dame has been painted as often as any building in the world; but . . . in the mere look and substance of a blind wall or a half-effaced advertisement, there can be found the materials not only of art, but of a lifetime of rewarded curiosity."

The Irish writer James Joyce—a pathbreaker, like Picasso, into the twentieth century—wrote to a friend from Paris in 1920: "There is an atmosphere of spiritual effort here. No other city is quite like it. It is a racecourse tension. I wake early, often at five o'clock, and start writing at once." Two years later, Joyce would publish his landmark novel *Ulysses*.

Picasso was fortunate in having several friends from Barcelona in Paris when he arrived. They had found him a studio previously used by another Spanish painter, Isidro Nonnel. Picasso set to work at once and soon made his first sale—three bullfight scenes bought by the art dealer Berthe Weill for 100 francs. (At that time, an artist could rent a studio for 15 francs a month, and one could live comfortably for 2 francs a day.)

A businessman from Barcelona, Pedro Mañach, took an interest in Picasso's work and offered to become his patron. Mañach made a proposal of 150 francs per month for all Picasso's paintings. The young artist was quick to accept the offer: he had arrived with more enthusiasm than money and had to make a living from his work.

Since he had promised to come home for Christmas, Picasso returned to Barcelona late in 1900. His friends from The Four Cats gave him a hero's welcome and staged an informal exhibition of his work, taping the unframed canvases to the walls. He was given the nickname "Little Goya." After Christmas, Picasso visited Madrid. There he founded the short-lived art magazine *Arte Jovan (Young Art)* with his friend Francisco Soler. They hoped to bring the new ideas of the Catalan intellectuals to the conservative Spanish capital. But after the magazine's second issue, Picasso's patron wrote to demand his return to Paris.

The year 1901 was extremely productive. Picasso was painting two and three pictures a day. "One must work, work," he often said. "I paint just as I breathe." His patron introduced him to the influential art dealer Ambroise Vollard, and Picasso had his first Paris show at Vollard's gallery. He exhibited seventy-five pictures, all of them experiments in the style of other artists of the day. Four influences were predominant, among them that of the Impressionists of the late nineteenth century, with their emphasis on pure color and light. This style focused on the sensation aroused in the artist by his first view (impression) of a landscape, which was translated onto a canvas by rapid brushwork so the artist could complete his painting before that impression faded. The result was an intense concentration on color and light, as captured by a much simpler and less "realistic" method of painting than the traditional approach.

Leaders of the Impressionist movement, which was at its peak during the 1870s and '80s, included the French artists Claude Monet, Camille Pissarro, Edgar Degas, Pierre Auguste Renoir, and Paul Cézanne. By about 1900, most of these artists were branching off in new directions. Human subjects replaced landscapes (except for Monet) as their primary focus.

Picasso was also influenced by Vincent Van Gogh, the brilliant Dutch artist; Paul Gauguin, whose primary interests were in primitive religion and folk art; and Henri de Toulouse-Lautrec, who broke with his wealthy French family to live and work in the shabby artist's quarter of Montmartre. His pictures of this cluttered hillside neighborhood made a deep impression on Picasso, who also drew inspiration from Montmartre's colorful cabarets, circus, and music halls.

The art critics of Paris reviewed Picasso's first show in glowing terms. One said simply, "Picasso is a painter, absolutely and beautifully." But in spite of such high praise, the twenty-year-old artist was having difficulty selling his paintings. His new works were too unusual and powerful for the public taste. They did not romanticize poverty, ugliness, or brutality. His patron, Mañach, was put off by them and withdrew his support. Picasso began to experience real poverty.

During his first winter in Paris, Picasso ran out of canvas, paper, and board on which to work. Lacking the money for new materials, he sometimes used the back of an existing picture to paint a new one. This is how the picture called *Little Girl with a Hat* came to be on the back of *Woman with a Chignon*. That same year, Picasso painted over an existing picture and reused the surface for the painting *Child with a Dove*. Fifty years later, this painting, then owned by Lady Aberconway of Great Britain, was X-rayed by the Courtauld Institute at her request. Beneath the picture was an earlier painting of a standing woman.

Art historian Hans Jaffé has called *Child with a Dove* the first sign of a new phase of Picasso's work, which would come to be called his Blue Period (1901-04). This period was named for the blue tones that dominated his paintings and created an atmosphere of loneliness and despair. His subjects were primarily the poor and the outcast.

As Jaffé explains, "The masters who served as Picasso's mentors in the early years of his career had

Dancing at a street cafe in Paris in 1934.

observed and set down the figures they painted with cool objectivity. Picasso had followed their example in his earliest works, but here, a new relationship is introduced between the figure observed and the observer: a relationship of human sympathy. The painter is deeply involved, wholeheartedly caught up in the object represented."

The hardships of Picasso's life at this time were reflected in his work. He had become familiar with hunger, cold, and the many humiliations of poverty firsthand. When he saw the poor people of Paris and Barcelona, it was with a new compassion and sense of solidarity with their sufferings. He had moved away from the brash self-confidence of the previous year, when he wrote over a self-portrait: *"Yo el rey"* ("I am the king").

When Picasso returned to Barcelona in the spring of 1901, a one-man show was organized by his friends at the *Sala Pares*. Those who came to see his work were impressed by its power and maturity. Miguel Utrillo's review praised Picasso's "spirit of observation, which does not pardon the weaknesses of the people of our time, and brings out even the beauties of the horrible."

Picasso's burden of poverty was both shared and lightened by a growing circle of friends in the two cities he called home. Among them was the Spanish tailor Soler, whom everyone called "Patches." Picasso paid him with paintings for new suits, as his father had once paid their landlord in Málaga.

One day a young stranger appeared at Picasso's Paris studio in a state of breathless excitement. His name was Max Jacob, and he was an aspiring poet from Brittany who worked as a clerk, tutor, and art critic. He had just seen some of Picasso's work at Vollard's gallery and rushed out to find the artist "so that we could become friends." Such enthusiasm was hard to resist, and the two did become friends—for a lifetime, as it turned out.

Another new friend was the French poet Guillaume Apollinaire, who had a profound insight into the work that Picasso was doing at this time. He understood the universal sadness of the Blue Period paintings. "Picasso," said Apollinaire, "has looked at the human images floating in the blue of our memories. How unearthly they are, these skies . . . these lights."

Picasso's friend Sabartés also wrote a memorable description of Picasso's intense power of concentration—a power essential to true creativity. "His attention is torn between canvas and palette," wrote Sabartés, "but it never leaves either. Both stand in his line of sight, and he discerns them together. He gives himself body and soul to the work, as if in the grip of a spell."

During the winter of 1902-03, Picasso had his second show in Paris. It was another critical triumph, but still no one was buying pictures. He was sharing a room with Max Jacob, and sometimes they had to heat it by burning piles of Picasso's drawings because there was no money for fuel.

That winter, Picasso made his last visit to Barcelona before settling permanently in Paris. When he returned, he and Jacob moved into a rickety old tenement in Montmartre. Max called it the *Bateau Lavoir*—the Laundry Boat—because it looked like one of the river barges where working-class women washed their clothes. The building stood in the Rue Ravignan, and around the corner was a gray house with a large window facing north, for good, consistent light. There Picasso had his studio.

Max had trouble sleeping, and he would sometimes wander around Paris all night—perhaps to get away from the cramped quarters he shared with Picasso. The building had a damp, stale smell; the walls were dirty and spotted; and the floorboards wobbled under one's feet. Water had to be carried from a fountain in the courtyard. Picasso swore that the building held together only by force of habit.

Downstairs from the studio lived a grocer, who objected strongly to the noisy parties Picasso and his friends threw. "One night," recalled Picasso, "when Max and Apollinaire and all the gang were in my studio, we were making so much noise over Soriol's head that he couldn't sleep. He shouted up to us, 'Hey, . . . how about letting the honest workers sleep!' I started to bang on the floor—his ceiling—with a big stick and Max ran around shouting, 'Soriol, the big mouth! Soriol, the big mouth!' We kept up our racket long enough for him to figure out that he'd have been far better off without protest. He never gave us any trouble after that."

Apollinaire was a heavy drinker, and when Max made fun of him at one of their parties, he flew into a rage and chased his tormenter around the table. "I think Apollinaire was Max's favorite target," said Picasso. "He could always be sure of getting a rise out of him."

Near-sighted Jaimé Sabartés also came in for his share of abuse from Picasso and Max Jacob. One day they gave Sabartés their last few coins and told him to go buy an egg and whatever else he could find for so little money. On his way back to their room with the egg, some sausages, and a piece of bread, Sabartés fell on the stairs and broke the egg. "Pablo was furious," recalled Françoise Gilot, who was told about the incident by the painter.

> "You'll never amount to anything," he told him. "We give you our last penny and you can't even get back here with a whole egg. You'll be a failure all your life!" He grabbed up a fork and plunged it into one of the sausages. The sausage burst. He tried the other one. The same thing happened. Sabartés, with his weak eyesight, had bought two sausages so old and so rotten that they exploded like a pair of balloons as soon as the tines of the fork penetrated the skin. Pablo and Max divided between them the bread Sabartés had bought. All Sabartés got for his trouble was the bawling-out.

It was the kind of scene that would be repeated many times between the hot-tempered artist and his long-suffering friend. But Sabartés was by no means the only person whom Picasso treated badly. In his relationships with women, he was notoriously unreliable and sometimes downright abusive. "For me, there are only two kinds of women," he boasted. "Goddesses and doormats."

Picasso created this mournful *Family Group* in 1904, at the end of his Blue Period.

The first woman Picasso became involved with in Paris was Fernande Olivier, whom he met at the fountain in the courtyard of the *Bateau Lavoir*. She was holding a cat, and he was attracted by her affinity for animals, which he shared. They had youth and poverty in common as well, and the young Frenchwoman soon became the volatile Spaniard's constant companion. She modeled for his paintings, and later for his early sculptures, and was well liked by his other friends. Apollinaire's lover, the painter Marie Laurencin, did a collective portrait of the four of them. Gertrude Stein called Pablo and Fernande "the Picassos."

Picasso made other new acquaintances in Montmartre, including an artist named Kees Van Dongen. The three Van Dongen children were always delighted to see the young Spanish painter, whom the youngest daughter called "Tablo."

Picasso was always fascinated by the imaginative world of childhood. The child in him entered fully into the plans and games of the children he met. With an artist's perception, he knew that play was a child's work—a way of testing and becoming part of the world around him or her. Picasso would not become a father until he was forty years old, but he made friends with children all his life. And he painted them with rare sensitivity. Eventually, his many pictures of his own four children would form a "Family Gallery," which he refused to part with during his lifetime.

Even during his poorest days, Picasso surrounded himself with pets. His love of animals was one of his most likable qualities. He collected stray dogs and cats from all over Paris and kept a tame white mouse, which lived in a dresser drawer. One day, when food was scarce in the house, a stray cat he had taken in came to *his* rescue. It returned from a prowl through the neighborhood trailing a long string of sausages!

By 1905 new artistic currents were flowing through Paris. A group of artists whom critics called the *Fauves* ("wild beasts") had just shown their paintings at the annual *Salon d'Automne*—the major exhibition held in Paris every fall. Their paintings were marked by the use of bold, often distorted, forms and vivid colors. Many critics and viewers were outraged, but Picasso saw much to admire in the work of the *Fauves*, who included Henri Matisse and Georges Rouault.

Matisse, born in 1869, had been strongly influenced by the Impressionist movement, which originated in nineteenth-century landscape painting. Then he began to concentrate on color as a structural (basic) element of his compositions rather than a decorative element. He simplified both line and color to achieve strong compositions and also applied these concepts to sculpture. There his concerns with space and form could be realized in three dimensions.

The greatest influence on both Matisse and Picasso (who would become close friends) was Paul Cézanne, who broke away from the Impressionists and was called the first Post-Impressionist artist. A native of Aix-en-Provence, where he was born in 1839, Cézanne became increasingly preoccupied with the search for pictorial form and space. He made countless studies of the Provençal landscape around Mont-Sainte-Victoire (which Picasso called "Cézanne's mountain"). He also painted detailed still lifes and compositions with nude human figures. In the process, he began to use the entire picture space in a daring new way. In effect, he "broke up" the flat surface of the canvas by using geometrical shapes—the cone, cylinder, cube, and others—as building blocks for the objects he painted.

By treating objects of nature, including trees, fruits, and human bodies, in these terms, Cézanne constructed a pictorial "new world." Rather than copying

Picasso in his Bateau Lavoir studio in 1908. Behind him are
several sculptures from New Caledonia which suggest the
influence of Primitivism on his work of this period.

reality, he created a new kind of reality that differed from both art and nature as they had been defined in the past. Matisse, who understood what Cézanne was trying to do, expressed it well when he said of his own work: "I must interpret nature and submit it to the spirit of the picture."

Picasso saw the great retrospective exhibition that included Cézanne's work in 1905, and he was overwhelmed by the possibilities of this new concept of space. At this time, his personal life, too, was changing for the better. His pictures were beginning to sell. His relationship with Fernande Olivier was stable and would last for another six years. He was ready to move from the sadness and solitude of his Blue Period into brighter colors and subjects.

The year 1905 was rich in creativity for Picasso, who once said, "The artist goes through states of fullness and emptiness." The fullness of his life at this time is reflected in the paintings of the Rose, or Circus, Period. They were inspired largely by the weekly performance of the *Cirque Medrano*, the circus held in Montmartre every Sunday. In a way, the ritual of the circus took the place, for Picasso, of the bullfights he had attended every weekend with his father when he was growing up. He thoroughly enjoyed the clowns, acrobats, bareback riders, and trapeze artists and admired the skill of their performances. He made many friends among the circus people and often went backstage to see them at their daily chores, rehearsals, and practices.

Picasso was struck by the contrast between the pageantry, illusion, and danger of the circus and the harsh realities of the performers' everyday life. Circus and carnival people have always forged strong ties with each other because they are constantly moving from place to place. Picasso understood the experience of being on the fringes of society, and his Rose Period portraits, such as *The Harlequin's Family* and *The Actor*, convey these feelings. He was especially drawn to the character of Harlequin, the "sad clown," who had his beginnings in the Italian *commedia dell'arte*, a popular form of comedy from the sixteenth to the eighteenth century that featured a set cast of characters. Traditionally, Harlequin appeared in white face powder and a diamond-patterned costume. Picasso often painted his own features on the white face of Harlequin, whose powder masked his true identity. This character would become a familiar symbol in Picasso's work, notably in the two versions of *Three Musicians* painted in 1921.

The circus animals, too, fascinated Picasso and appeared in such paintings as *The Bareback Rider*, *Young Boy Leading a Horse*, and *Boy with Dog*. Both his skill at draftsmanship (drawing) and his feeling for human and animal subjects are apparent in these pictures. One of the most beautiful paintings of this period is *Acrobat's Family with a Monkey*, in which the monkey is portrayed with such tenderness of feeling that it becomes a true member of its human family.

At the time of the circus paintings, Apollinaire had been helping the artist to become better known through his influence in the art world. In 1905 the American collector Leo Stein bought the picture *Young Girl with a Basket of Flowers*. Soon afterward, Stein and his sister Gertrude—already a well-known writer experimenting in new forms of expression—visited Picasso and purchased more of his paintings. Picasso soon became a member of the group that attended the Steins' *salons*—regular gatherings of artists and intellectuals.

In 1906 the Steins gave Picasso his first commission (payment to undertake a particular work). They asked him to do a portrait of Gertrude's nephew, Allan Stein. The painting was a success, and Picasso asked Gertrude to pose for him. Her strong features and commanding air proved harder to capture on canvas than her nephew's likeness. Stein sat for her portrait eighty times, and Picasso was still dissatisfied with his efforts. The sittings put a severe strain on their friendship, which was often stormy anyway: both had very domineering personalities. To their mutual disappointment, Picasso gave up on the portrait and destroyed all his work. Finally, he finished the painting from memory and presented it to the writer as a gift. During her lifetime, it hung in her Paris apartment in the Rue de Fleurus and is now in the collection of the Metropolitan Museum of Art in New York City.

Picasso's fortunes improved again when the art dealer Vollard offered to represent him and gave him 2,000 francs as an advance against future paintings. Encouraged, Picasso left Paris for a painting holiday at Gosol in the Pyrenees. The pictures he worked on there and after his return to Paris showed two new and important influences. One was that of the ancient Iberian bronze sculptures he had seen in Spain (which was called Iberia in Roman times). The other was his recent discovery of African sculpture in Paris's Trocadero Museum. He was attracted by its primitive power, bold distortions of nature, and deep sense of mystery.

The African masks and sculptures suggested a new way of seeing the human form—from several sides at once, rather than from the fixed perspective of tradition. These visions were at war with one another, and the conflict broke out in a revolutionary painting that shocked Picasso's critics, friends, and fellow artists alike.

Violin (1915), an assemblage constructed out of pieces of metal.

CHAPTER 4

CUBISM

In 1907 Picasso began work on his breakthrough painting—a picture so large that he had to rent the high-ceilinged loft of his studio building to undertake it. He made numerous studies for this canvas, which was almost eight feet square, and worked on it over a long period of time. The creative struggle in which he was engaged is apparent in the painting's final form.

Les Demoiselles d'Avignon (The Young Women of Avignon) has been called the first true twentieth-century painting because of its revolutionary role in the history of art. The title was not Picasso's—he never titled his works—but that of a viewer who thought the painting resembled a scene from a house of prostitution in Barcelona's red-light district, Avignon Street. Five women are depicted in the painting, which has a still life of fruit in the foreground. The movement from past to future is seen in the contrast between the three figures on the left and the two on the right. The women on the left are not unlike traditional studies of the human form, even though strong distortions and geometrical structure give them a startling new look. But the figures on the right are a total break with the past. Their faces are angular and stylized, like those of the African masks. Most importantly, the body in the foreground is presented from several sides at once. Cézanne's influence is seen in the geometric angles and planes that would lead the critics to call Picasso's new style "Cubist."

At first, the term "Cubism" was used in a spirit of hostility and rejection. As H. W. Jansen points out in *History of Art*, in this painting "Picasso used primitive art as a battering ram against the classical conception of beauty." His new view of the human body was so disturbing that one critic said of the canvas, "It resembles a field of broken glass." Even friends like Leo Stein called the new painting "monstrous." The only person who believed in it was a young German-born art dealer named Daniel-Henry Kahnweiler, who had just opened a gallery in the Rue Vignon. Profoundly impressed by the work, he offered to represent Picasso. This was the beginning of a lifelong business and personal relationship that endured despite many ups and downs. (Picasso was as unpredictable with his dealers as he was with his friends and often pitted them against each other to get the best prices for his work.) But Kahnweiler's loyalty remained unswerving from the time he saw *Les Demoiselles*. Years later, he would say of those days: "What I should like to make you feel is the incredible heroism of a man like

Picasso, whose moral solitude at the time was something terrifying. Not one of his painter friends had followed his lead. [Georges] Braque, who had met Picasso through Apollinaire, declared that to him it seemed as if someone had drunk kerosene and started spitting fire."

But Braque, too, had been deeply impressed by the African works discovered by the *Fauves*. He began to collect African art, and eventually he was won over to Picasso's bold experiment. They began to work together in the Cubist style, and for several years their paintings developed along parallel lines. In fact, the two were so closely allied that their works were sometimes hard to tell apart. Other artists began to follow their lead. Forty years later, Braque would say of those exciting years: "We lived in Montmartre, we saw each other every day, we talked a lot. We were like two mountain climbers roped together. We both of us worked very hard. The museums had no more interest for us. We went to some exhibitions, but not so many. Above all, we were wholly wrapped up in our work."

By 1910 Picasso's name was known internationally; he had achieved a degree of recognition almost unheard of for an artist not yet thirty years old. The Cubist landscapes he painted at Horta de Ebro, the village of Pallarés, in 1909 have been described as "a systematic re-creation of reality." They confirmed his reputation as the key figure in the evolution of modern art. And financial success came with artistic recognition, which is not always the case. Picasso would never be poor again.

During this time, Picasso crossed the sharp line that had once separated painting and sculpture. His Cubist sculptures, including several heads of Fernande Olivier, carried his experiments in form to a new level.

In this bursting of limits, he was a pioneer. As Robert Goldwater points out, "The former demarcations between the arts no longer held good." Picasso would prove it—in such a variety of styles and materials that it is difficult to believe they are the work of a single person.

Gertrude Stein mentioned Picasso's new prosperity in her book *The Autobiography of Alice B. Toklas* (Stein's long-time companion). "The Picassos," she wrote, "moved from their old studio in the Rue Ravignan to an apartment in the Boulevard Clichy. Fernande began to buy furniture and have a servant. [She] had at this time a new friend of whom she often spoke to me. This was Eve, who was living with Marcoussis. One evening all four of them came to the Rue de Fleurus, Pablo, Fernande, Marcoussis and Eve. I could perfectly understand Fernande's liking for Eve."

Unfortunately for Fernande, Picasso also found her new friend extremely attractive. Within a short time, he had broken off his relationship with Fernande and formed one with Eve Gouel. Stein had described Eve as "small and perfect," and Picasso was very much in love with her. "I shall write her name on my pictures," he said to Kahnweiler. The series of paintings called *Ma Jolie* (My Darling) were a tribute to Eve.

About 1912 Picasso and Braque began to experiment with the idea of using objects and materials from everyday life in their paintings. These materials included paper, cloth, sand, rope—whatever could form part of a collage with the familiar artistic materials of paint and canvas. One of the best-known early examples of Collage Cubism is the composition *Still Life with Chair Caning* , in which an abstract still life seems to rest on an object—the chair caning—and the whole is encircled by a rope. In effect, the picture looks as if it were resting on a tray. The traditional idea of "picture space" was challenged.

Later, Picasso would discuss Collage Cubism with Françoise Gilot, who recorded their talks in *Life with Picasso*. Referring to the works he and Braque had produced between 1912 and 1914, he said, "If a piece of newspaper can become a bottle, that gives us something to think about in connection with both newspapers and bottles, too. The displaced object has entered a universe for which it is not made, and it retains, in a measure, its strangeness. And this strangeness was what we wanted to make people think about."

Other artists, too, were starting to link art and life in their works. The French artist Marcel Duchamp was moving from Cubist painting into the construction of "Readymades"—mass-produced commercial objects chosen by the artist. His *Bicycle Wheel*, which was just that, posed a new challenge for the critics. As one art historian put it: "If the artist is no longer depicting reality, but instead using parts of that reality as parts of his picture, how can you decide what a work of art should be?" Duchamp's answer was that you could not. In effect, he denied the possibility of defining art in the traditional way. This placed him with Picasso, Braque, and a growing number of others who had moved decisively into the field of modern art.

When World War I broke out in Europe in 1914, Picasso was living in an elegant studio in the Rue Schoelcher. As he was a Spanish national and Spain was not involved in the war, he was able to stay in Paris. But most of his French friends, including Max Jacob, were drafted into the army or volunteered for service. Despite the improvement in his living conditions, it was not a completely happy time for Picasso. As Stein recalled it, "The only excitement was the letters from Guillaume Apollinaire, who was falling off of horses in the endeavor to become an artilleryman."

During the second year of the war, Eve Gouel died of tuberculosis while Picasso was on a trip to the Spanish island of Majorca. Saddened by this loss, and by the absence of his friends, Picasso gave up the studio in the Rue Schoelcher and moved out to the suburb of Montrouge. Here he returned to a realistic style of painting for the first time in eight years. Side by side with his Cubist paintings were precise, lifelike drawings and portraits. In part, this was a personal reaction to the war years. But it was also part of the general reaction against change that overtook Europe at this time and continued into the postwar period.

Four years of widespread chaos and destruction turned people's minds to the past and what was best

Marcel Duchamp took the Cubist ideas into Readymade art, which asks the question "How can you decide what a work of art should be?"

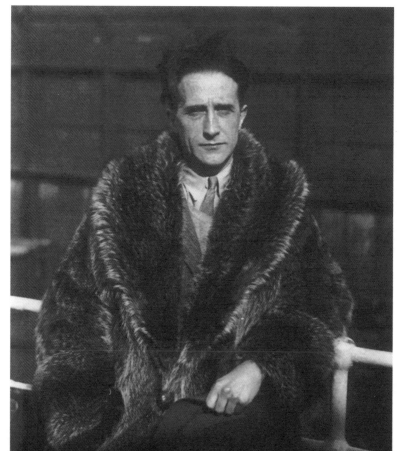

about it. There was a feeling that Western civilization had been deeply threatened—in fact, had barely survived—and this led to a collective search for cultural roots. Suddenly, there was a newfound appreciation for tradition, which had been out of favor since before the turn of the century. As Janson explains it, "Without tradition—the word means 'that which has been handed to us'—no originality would be possible. It provides, as it were, the firm platform from which the artist makes his leap of the imagination. The place where he lands will then become part of the web and serve as a point of departure for further leaps."

In Picasso's case, the return to tradition was reinforced by marriage and the birth of a child—events that affirm the value and continuity of human life in spite of danger and discouragement. In 1916, while working on scenery and costumes for the ballet *Parade*, at the invitation of French poet Jean Cocteau, Picasso met a graceful young Russian dancer named Olga Koklova. She was a member of the Russian Ballet company headed by Sergei Diaghilev, a world-famous impresario.

His work on *Parade* exposed Picasso to people who lived a far more glamorous social life than most of his former associates. Some of the members of the Russian Ballet came from wealthy families; Olga was a member of the minor Russian nobility. Those who were not outstanding dancers were included in the company because they would attract people from their own social set. For a time, at least, Picasso was caught up in the ambitions for status that swirled around him. He believed the beautiful young dancer would enhance his prestige among his new associates, and he asked her to marry him. It was an ill-judged partnership, as Olga knew nothing about painting and Picasso really cared little for the kind of "high life" she represented. Nevertheless, he brought her to Barcelona to meet his family.

Even Picasso's mother tried to dissuade Olga from marrying him. "You poor girl," she said to the bride-to-be. "You don't know what you're letting yourself in for. If I were a friend I would tell you not to do it under any conditions. I don't believe any woman could be happy with my son. He's available for himself but for no one else."

Unfortunately, Doña Maria was very accurate in her predictions of an unhappy marriage. But her advice was ignored: Olga and Picasso were married in 1917, the year before the war ended. And Olga's idea of a social life soon proved both boring and distracting to her husband. One of Picasso's dealers, Paul Rosenberg, found the couple an apartment in the Rue la Boétie, but it had no studio. After an unsuccessful attempt to work in a large room, Picasso rented the apartment above them for working space and solitude. Even so, his time was taken up with a steady round of masquerades, fancy-dress balls, and holidays in the south of France with the restless "lost generation" (those Americans who were disillusioned with their own country and chose to live in France after World War I).

During this period, Picasso met many American artists and writers who gravitated toward Gertrude Stein's *salons*. This group included the American novelist F. Scott Fitzgerald, author of *The Great Gatsby*, and his beautiful wife Zelda. Both were known for their hard drinking and high living. Another promising young writer from the United States was Ernest Hemingway, who wrote *The Sun Also Rises* and *A Movable Feast* from his experiences in Paris during the 1920s.

Picasso's settings and costumes for the ballet *Parade* were enormously successful. After that, he was

One of the studies sketched by the artist in 1919 before executing the drop curtain for the ballet *The Three-Cornered Hat.*

invited to collaborate on the London production of a ballet with a Spanish theme: *The Three-Cornered Hat.* Composer Manuel de Falla provided the music, and Picasso designed a drop curtain with a bullring scene.

While working on this ballet, Picasso made his second visit to Rome, where he was deeply impressed by the monumental sculptures of the classical age. Their influence is apparent in the 1921 painting *Three Women at the Spring*, with its huge stonelike figures.

Picasso's first child, Paulo, was born in 1921 when the artist was forty years old. The theme of mother and child had always been attractive to Picasso. He began a series of drawings and paintings in his new Neoclassic style, with Olga and Paulo as his subjects. From 1921 through 1925, he made many paintings—called *Maternitiés*—with the mother-and-child theme. His Family Gallery also included portraits of Paulo alone, including two famous pictures of his son in circus costume, as Harlequin and as Pierrot, the comic yet pathetic mime character who wore an oversize white clown suit. All three of these portraits are now in the collection of the Picasso Museum in Paris.

However, once the novelty of parenthood wore off, and his son began to interfere with his work, Picasso withdrew from Paulo as he had from his wife. The constant bustle of nursemaids for the child and house-maids and cooks for the apartment got on his nerves, and he spent more and more time alone in his studio or with his friends. As he once said to another woman in his life: "Everybody has the same energy potential. The average person wastes his in a dozen little ways. I bring mine to bear on one thing only: my painting. Everything is sacrificed to it—you and everyone else, myself included."

One result of his parents' frequent absences was that Paulo spent much of his time with the family servants. His particular favorite was the chauffeur, Marcel, who worked for Picasso for twenty-five years. Paulo began to imitate Marcel's way of speaking and even his walk. He became fascinated with cars and

Portrait of Olga Koklova (1916), Picasso's first wife.

motorcycles at the age of four or five, and this interest persisted throughout his adolescence. It was a source of constant friction with his father, who was always pushing him to do well in school, and, later, to get work. In fact, Marcel often acted as go-between for Paulo with his father, even into the boy's early manhood.

During his son's infancy, Picasso continued to break new ground in his painting. In 1921 he produced two major works, both entitled *The Three Musicians*. The influence of his theater work with the ballet was apparent in the bright colors and dramatic portrayal of the musicians, one of whom was dressed as Harlequin. These pictures are considered a high point in the style of Collage Cubism. They are so skillfully painted in the "cut-paper style" that one cannot readily tell whether they are painted or pasted. In fact, no pasted materials were used.

During the mid-1920s, the various styles in which Picasso had been working began to come together. This merging tendency can be seen in the 1925 painting *Woman with Mandolin*, which combines Cubist and classical styles. Color plays a more dominant role than it had in earlier Cubist paintings. Here, there is a harmonious blending of white, blue, and red, rather than the darker shades of such pictures as the landscapes at Horta de Ebro and the musical instruments of the previous decade.

About 1925 Picasso's work took a turn into the magic of myth and legend. Seven years into the postwar period, society was beginning to lose faith in the possibility of a return to traditional ways and the old order of things. The calmness and control of the classical style was being questioned again, as men and women doubted that reason alone could form the basis of a lasting society.

In art, the Surrealists ("super realists") showed this anti-reason spirit through dreamlike works in which nothing was what it seemed to be. Recent discoveries about the unconscious mind, as it showed itself in dreams and symbols, formed part of the Surrealist Manifesto written by André Breton in Paris in 1924. Originally a literary movement, Surrealism soon came to exert a major influence on artists like Salvador Dali, a Spanish painter who became the best-known member of the movement.

Picasso, too, was affected by Surrealism, but he followed his own path in attempting to express the emerging spirit of the time. The 1925 painting *The Three Dancers* marks a turning point in his art. In this powerful painting, the distortions and wild gestures of the dancers create a sense of ecstasy—of being carried totally out of oneself by a transcendent experience. The picture conveys both a passion for life and an affirmation that life is more than the mind alone can tell us. What is captured here is another dimension of the human spirit.

Maïa with a Doll (1938). Picasso never tired of painting children.

CHAPTER 5

YEARS OF GROWTH AND CONFLICT

$\mathbf{A}$s so often was the case with Picasso's work, *The Three Dancers* was a bridge to new experiments in art. As soon as the critics and the public thought they understood Picasso, he surprised them again. By refusing to be imprisoned in a single style or vision, he committed himself to the risk of constant growth and change. This process went on throughout his career—a period of more than seventy years. As he said himself, "Basically, I am perhaps a painter without style."

Picasso's lifelong interest in the creative process was expressed in many paintings of the artist at work, the studio, and the artist and his model. Form remained his primary concern, and he looked for new ways to express its three dimensions on the two-dimensional canvas. In *The Painter and His Model* , color was reduced to a few shades of gray and tan, with a darker gray for shading. A network of curving lines over the whole picture space suggested depth. These techniques of drawing, or graphics, were characteristic of Picasso's work. During the mid-1920s they became even more apparent.

Storytelling is one of humanity's oldest ways of remembering the past and making sense of the human experience. At this time, Picasso renewed his artistic ties to myth and legend. He showed a special interest in changes of form—called metamorphoses. In 1930 he made a series of etchings to illustrate a new edition of *The Metamorphoses* by the Latin poet Ovid. These classic poems described the changes of form that various persons and things had undergone since the world emerged from Chaos—a state of universal formlessness and confusion. The book had provided subject matter for artists since the time of Julius Caesar, and the fast-changing twentieth century gave new meaning to Ovid's stories.

Another important work of 1930 was the painting *The Crucifixion*, in which the tiny figure of a *picador* holds up a lance to the side of the crucified figure. The theme of pain and death, tied closely to the bullfight ritual, would appear repeatedly during the 1930s. This was a troubled time, both in Picasso's personal life and in the world. In Germany, the National Socialist (Nazi) Party, led by Adolf Hitler, was coming to power. Its long-range plans included the domination of all Europe and the ruthless destruction of any person or group that opposed it. A worldwide economic depression had affected millions, causing widespread poverty, homelessness, and lack of work. In the Far East, the Japanese Empire, Asia's leading power, was moving aggressively against China. There was growing uneasiness about the shape of political events around the world.

For several years, Picasso's marriage to Olga had been strained and unhappy. During the early 1930s the two separated, and the artist went through a personal crisis that he described as "a season in hell." Some biographers say that he even stopped painting for a while. At this time he bought a large country house, the Château de Boisgeloup, where his friend Julio González taught him how to make sizable welded sculptures in metal. Over the next few years, Picasso produced about fifty large sculptures, many from plaster or wooden models that were later cast in bronze. These included variations on the head of a woman; tall, thin human figures called "stick-statuettes"; and animal figures, including a rooster and a young cow.

At the same time, Picasso was involved in a new type of sculpture: the assemblage of actual objects and raw materials into three-dimensional constructions. Art historian Roland Penrose has described Picasso's use of these "found objects," as they are called, with amusement and insight:

> Pieces of scrap-iron, springs, saucepan lids, sieves, bolts and screws picked out with discernment from the rubbish heap, could mysteriously take their place in these constructions, wittily and convincingly coming to life with a new personality. The vestiges of their origins remained visible as witnesses to the transformation that the magician had brought about, a challenge to the identity of anything and everything.

The paintings Picasso worked on during this time are closely related to his experiments in sculpture. They, too, have a magical quality. Rounded shapes and free-flowing lines predominate. His model was Marie-Thérèse Walter, the subject of the 1932 painting

Woman Asleep in a Red Armchair, also called *The Dream*.
This was one of many pictures of seated or reclining
women asleep.

Perhaps the best-known picture of this period is
Girl Before a Mirror. This striking portrait of a young
woman gazing into a mirror is done in rich colors of
red, yellow, green, and blue with dark, heavy lines
that give it the look of stained glass.

Picasso's reputation was still growing. In 1932
large retrospective exhibitions of his work were held
in Paris and Zurich, Switzerland. The artist had mixed
feelings about such recognition. In fact, he once said,
"Success is dangerous. One begins to copy oneself,
and to copy oneself is more dangerous than to copy
others." But by now his standing as a major artist was
unquestioned, whether or not one liked his work. Like
all artists, Picasso had his critics, but popularity was
not his concern. As he said of his Cubist work in an
interview for *The Arts* magazine: "The fact that for a
long time Cubism has not been understood means
nothing. I do not read English: an English book is a
blank book to me. This does not mean that the English
language does not exist, and why should I blame
anybody else but myself if I cannot understand what I
know nothing about?"

In 1934, a visit to Spain gave Picasso a new vision
of the bullfight as a symbol of the times. In his sketchbooks the bull began to appear as a sign of rage, pos-
sessed by enormous power. The following year, he
combined the symbols of bull and Minotaur in the
etching *Minotauromachy*.

In 1935 Picasso's marriage ended in divorce. In
October, his daughter Maïa was born to his model
Marie-Thérèse Walter. The long and unhappy relationship between painter and model would continue
for many years, although the two rarely shared a

Crucifixion (1930) was not a religious painting, but rather depicted human anguish and suffering.

home. Maïa, whose full name was Maria de la Concepción, was the subject of many paintings, including *Maïa with Her Doll.* These pictures became part of Picasso's personal collection until his death.

The summer of 1936 brought disastrous news from Picasso's homeland. Civil war had broken out between supporters of the Spanish Republic and conservatives who wanted to restore the Spanish monarchy. The Spanish government had been unstable for years, and a Republican victory in elections held early in 1936 led to violence on both sides.

The armed forces, monarchists, aristocrats, and Roman Catholic officials were all hostile to the Republican government in Madrid, which had tried to introduce liberal reforms. An army general named Francisco Franco set up a dictatorship in Burgos in October 1936, in opposition to the Spanish Republic, and the stage was set for almost three years of brutal conflict throughout Spain.

Franco received aid from Nazi Germany and the oppressive fascist government of Italy, where Benito Mussolini had become a dictator. In April 1937, the Spanish dictator ordered German planes to bomb the northern town of Guernica. It was the capital of the Basque region, which shared the independent spirit of Catalonia. Such independence was a threat to the dictatorship of Franco, which was known for its forcible supression of the opposition.

The bombing of Guernica was an act of pure terrorism, as the town had no military importance. It was totally destroyed. The defenseless civilian population was massacred by the German planes. The destruction of Guernica foreshadowed the horrors of modern warfare that would occur during World War II, which would begin two years later.

Picasso had spoken out in favor of the Republican cause as soon as the Civil War began. The government, in turn, had named him director of the national museum, the Prado. This honor was combined with the request that Picasso paint a mural—a wall-size picture—for the Spanish Pavillion at the World Exposition in Paris. It was scheduled to begin in June 1937. When Guernica was destroyed in April, Picasso picked total warfare as his theme. He began making studies for the mural as fast as he could: within weeks he had completed sixty of them. By early June, the 26-foot painting, almost 12 feet high, was finished and installed in the Spanish Pavillion to international acclaim.

Picasso's painting *Guernica* was done in the Collage Cubist style and was painted entirely in black, white, and gray. The starkness of its tones added intensity to its powerful images of war. On the left, a human-headed bull looms over an anguished woman holding a dead child. Below them is the outstretched arm of a fallen fighter, whose right hand clutches a broken sword. (This was a familiar symbol for heroic resistance to an enemy of superior force.)

At the center of the painting is the shocked face of a woman holding a lamp, who suggests Liberty, and a distorted human figure gazing at a dying horse—a victim of mindless destruction. On the right is an agonized figure with arms flung up toward a tiny window that lets in a square of light. Every figure in the painting, except that of the dead child, has its mouth open as if in a scream.

Those who saw the painting at the Paris World Exhibition were deeply disturbed by its warning about the full-scale destruction made possible by the weapons and practices of modern warfare. World War I had seen the introduction of trench warfare, poison gas, barbed wire, tanks, submarines, and planes. That war had almost destroyed a generation of young men from England, France, and Germany—the major participants in the war, which was fought entirely on European soil and waters. Although the United States did not enter the war until 1917, many Americans were killed in the remaining year of the conflict. In short, the world had learned that war would never be the same again—a matter of set battles between professional armies, fought largely away from civilian populations. In fact, World War I had been described as

Guernica, Picasso's monumental anti-war painting, was first
exhibited at the Spanish Pavillion of the 1937 World Exposition in
Paris. It expresses the artist's outrage at the destruction of the town
of Guernica by the air force of Nazi Germany, then allied with
General Franco during the Spanish Civil War. Guernica was the
capital of the Basque province, an area of Spain with a strong

separatist movement. By raining terror on an unsuspecting
civilian population, Franco callously sought to crush the spirit of
those who resisted him. The Nazis, on the other hand, viewed the
Spanish conflict as a prelude to World War II and used it to
demonstrate their air superiority.

Francisco Franco *(inset)* led the fascists in their takeover of Spain during the Spanish Civil War (1936-1939). *(Above)* The town of Teruel, in Aragon Province, was the scene of a particularly bloody battle where 15,000 people were killed.

Night Fishing at Antibes (1939) was painted one month before World War II began. The conflict would shatter peaceful scenes such as this.

"the war to end all war." The League of Nations had been formed after the armistice to ensure world peace for the future. But such a union depended upon cooperation, and the 1930s had already proved that such cooperation was hard to come by.

For the next several years, as the world moved closer to world war, echoes of *Guernica* rang through Picasso's work. Other paintings of the late 1930s included the powerful *Weeping Woman*, the menacing *Woman Dressing Her Hair*, in which a huge, frightening female figure dominates the canvas, and *Night Fishing at Antibes*, completed the month before World War II began. *Night Fishing* has been interpreted as a chilling contrast between the normalcy of everyday life and the destruction to come.

Like *Guernica*, *Night Fishing at Antibes* is a large picture—about 11 by 7 feet. It was painted at the French port of Antibes, where Picasso was staying during the summer of 1939. On the right side of the painting, two girls with a bicycle and an ice-cream cone look on from a seawall at the central figures—two brutish looking fishermen in a small boat. One scans the depths while the other spears a fish. This night scene is lit by torches, which appear in the painting as brilliant starlike objects. At the top left rise the purplish towers of the Grimaldi Castle. Picasso would live there for a time after the war. When he gave the town a gift of paintings and ceramics, it became the Picasso Museum of Antibes. Art historian Alfred H. Barr, Jr., has called *Night Fishing at Antibes* one of Picasso's major works of the decade following *Guernica*, his best-known painting.

In 1939 Barr was instrumental in organizing a major retrospective called "Picasso: Forty Years of His Art" at the Museum of Modern Art in New York City. It included more than 300 works and was seen at museums all over the United States. For many years, *Guernica* could be seen at the Museum of Modern Art. It was on indefinite loan from the artist. But some years after his death, and the death of Franco, it was returned to Spain.

The year 1939 brought many personal losses to Picasso. His mother died in Barcelona on January 13, two weeks before the city surrendered to Franco's forces. In March, the capital, Madrid, fell to fascist forces and the Republicans were finally defeated. From this time on, Picasso would never return to Spain. He refused to enter his homeland while it was controlled by Franco's fascist dictatorship and remained in self-exile for the rest of his life. Then that July his longtime friend Ambroise Vollard, who had sponsored his first exhibition in France, was killed in an automobile accident. And September brought events that would affect the entire world.

Weeping Woman (1937) The poet Eluard said that this portrait of
Dora Maar reminded him of someone who "had found herself
suddenly faced by a heart-rending disaster."

CHAPTER 6

THE WAR YEARS

By the fall of 1939, several Central European countries had been swallowed up by Nazi Germany. Aus-
tria was now part of the Third Reich, as Hitler called
his dictatorship of Germany. The industrial Ruhr
Valley, over which Germany had lost control after its
defeat in World War I, was reoccupied by Hitler's
armies. This area would be valuable to the war effort
because of its natural resources, such as coal and
metal.

Czechoslovakia had been taken over with little
opposition from Western Europe's democratic powers,
Great Britain and France. These countries had suffered so many losses in World War I that they were

very slow to resist Hitler's aggressions. Everyone hoped that the problem would simply go away. But when Germany made a surprise attack on Poland on September 1, Western Europe had to take a stand; its alliance with the Eastern European country demanded it. And it had become only too clear that Nazi Germany had to be stopped. England and France declared war on Germany.

Western Europe was alone in the fight since the leaders of Nazi Germany and the Soviet Union had signed a secret agreement not to go to war with each other. A state of suspense prevailed for the next six months, during which Germany overran British and allied naval forces to seize part of the Scandinavian peninsula. The countries of Norway and Denmark were occupied by the Germans, whose submarines were also winning the naval war in the Atlantic. Then Hitler broke his agreement with the dictator of the Soviet Union, Joseph Stalin, by launching a surprise attack across Soviet borders in June 1941, causing the Soviets to enter the war on the side of the Allies.

The United States would not enter the war until December 1941, after Japan allied itself with Nazi Germany and attacked the U.S. Pacific Fleet at Pearl Harbor, Hawaii. But American sympathies were with England and France, and the nation watched anxiously during the spring of 1940 as German tanks, planes, and submarines moved toward Western Europe. The Germans took over the small countries of Holland and Belgium, in spite of courageous resistance, and entered France on May 12. Conflict and confusion in the French military command, plus the strength and speed of the German invasion, led to the rapid defeat of France. The French line of defense on the west—called the Maginot Line—was thought to be invincible, but the Germans broke through it quickly. France was occupied by enemy forces.

Picasso had been staying at the seaside town of Royan, but he returned to his studio in Paris, despite many invitations to leave the country and find safety overseas. He felt a deep loyalty to France because it had been his home for some 35 years and because he could not return to his own country. So he shared the dangers and distress of the Occupation for the next four years. Personal freedom was severely restricted, and the French people lived in fear. The Germans searched constantly for members of the French Resistance—secret freedom fighters who tried to drive out the invaders. They blew up railroad tracks and bridges to prevent German armies and supplies from entering the country. They spied on Nazi officers and made surprise attacks based on the information they had gathered. Anyone who was found to be hiding a member of the Resistance, or a Jewish man, woman, or child, was imprisoned and faced possible torture and execution.

Sometimes a whole village would be terrorized by Nazi storm troopers searching for members of the Resistance. Even if none was found, village leaders might be rounded up and shot as an example of what would happen to those who resisted the Occupation. One's home could be taken over without warning, and it was impossible to travel freely from place to place. French Jews were at as much risk as members of the Resistance. They could be arrested at a moment's notice, their businesses and belongings confiscated, and their families deported to death camps, which were described as work camps to prevent widespread terror and organized revolt.

These were terrible years for France, and Great Britain was in grave danger of falling to the Nazi forces too. German planes made raids on British towns and cities for weeks on end, trying to bomb the island nation into submission. Members of the Royal

Air Force (RAF) were flying two and three missions a day to intercept and shoot down enemy planes. The United States offered all the help it could without actually entering the war, but German submarines, or U-boats (underwater boats), made travel and shipping dangerous throughout the Atlantic Ocean. Fascist Italy had come into the war on the German side, and Japan soon joined these Axis powers, as they were called. Finally, after the bombing of Pearl Harbor, the United States entered the war, fighting both in Europe against Germany and Italy and in the Pacific Ocean against Japan.

It was war on a scale the world had never dreamed of, with weapons of inconceivable power. Not until after the war would its full scope be understood—the millions of lives lost and the billions of dollars worth of property destroyed. The historic German city of Dresden would be completely devastated by fire bombs. London and other British cities would suffer great damage during the "blitz" of German bombing, but would resist long enough to prevent a full-scale invasion. Thousands of American seamen and many great battleships would be lost at Pearl Harbor and in the battles that succeeded it: Iwo Jima, Guadalcanal, the Coral Sea, the Solomon Islands. Other unfamiliar names would become known around the world as synonyms for the mass torment and murder of the Jewish people and other victims of the Nazis: Dachau, Bergen-Belsen, Auschwitz.

Throughout these years, Picasso worked in his studio at 7 Rue de Augustins despite shortages of food, fuel, and art materials. He did not paint the war as such. But his pictures and sculptures reflected the trauma through which the world was passing. In such paintings as *Seated Woman in Blue*, the distorted figure of the woman appears to be imprisoned by the arms of

The Nazis marched into Paris on June 14, 1940.

the chair. There is a sense of powerless struggle against some force too great to be overcome.

Another series of wartime paintings returned to the symbol of the bull as a figure of death: there were many versions of *Still Life with Bull's Head*, including one with a bull's skull. Both animal and human skulls appear frequently in the work of this period. But there were also signs of optimism about the future. In 1942 Picasso began a long series of drawings of a rugged shepherd carrying a sheep, which would become the armature (framework) for a 7-foot major sculpture by 1944.

Picasso also expressed himself in other ways during this period. He wrote a Surrealist play entitled *Desire Trapped by the Tail*, which was performed privately at the home of his friends Michel and Louise Leiris. The play centered on the theme of transformation—objects turned into human figures, and events followed one another without any rational explanation.

The theme of change appeared again in the assemblage *Bull's Head*, in which an old bicycle seat became the animal's head and a set of handlebars its horns. (This work was later cast in bronze.) When friends admired it, Picasso said simply:

> That is all very well. But the bull's head should have been thrown away immediately afterwards. Thrown into the street, into the gutter. Then a working man would come along and pick it up. And he would find that out of this bull's head he might be able to make a bicycle seat and handlebars. And he does so. Now *that* would have been wonderful. That is the gift of metamorphosis.

The Germans offered Picasso special privileges because of his fame and because he was Spanish by birth rather than French. Spain didn't fight in the war, but it did aid the Axis countries economically. It is

Bull's Head (1943) was created out of the handlebars and seat of a bicycle. Picasso commented, "I made a bull's head, which everybody recognized as a bull's head. Thus a metamorphosis was completed."

said that the Germans once offered to allow him more fuel than others received, and he advised them that "a Spaniard is never cold." There must have been more pride than truth in the statement because all Paris was cold during the years of the Occupation. On another occasion, a group of German officers came to his studio to see his work, and he presented them with photographs of *Guernica* (postcards of the painting had been made up and sold to support the Republican cause).

"Did you do this?" asked one of the officers.

"No," replied Picasso. "You did."

One of the most powerful images of the war years

created by Picasso was a simple study of marching feet—drawn on newspaper because there was no drawing paper in Paris. But despite the scarcity of material, major works continued to emerge from Picasso's studio. In 1942 he completed thirty-one watercolors of various animals for an edition of Buffon's classic *Natural History*, published by the house of Fabiani. When the Germans ruled that all statues were to be melted down so that the metal could be used for military purposes, Picasso continued to cast his plaster models in bronze. His friend Sabartés urged him to do so. "Plaster is perishable," he warned. "Bronze is forever." Other friends helped him carry the plaster models to the foundry for casting at night, in handcarts, to avoid the German patrols. This must have pleased the sculptor Julio González, who had shared his skill with Picasso in the early 1930s. The death of González soon after the end of the war was another deeply felt loss.

Other friends were in grave danger. Paul Eluard, who had been a member of the Communist Party during the 1920s, rejoined it because it opposed the Nazis. He also worked with the French Resistance. The poet Max Jacob, Picasso's companion during the Laundry Boat days in Montmartre, was forced to wear the yellow star that the Germans used to identify all Jews. In 1944 he was arrested and sent to the concentration camp at Drancy, France, where he died of pneumonia within two weeks. Christian Zervos, who had catalogued all of Picasso's work since 1901 in thirteen volumes, was in hiding. The Germans had taken over his apartment without notice because of his close relationships with Picasso and artists whose work the Nazis had banned. (Zervos was Greek by birth, but he had lived in France for years and edited the influential art magazine *Cahiers d'Art*.) Picasso saw his remaining friends in his studio or in bistros like Le Catalan, where they gathered when they could.

On June 6, 1944, allied British and American forces crossed the English Channel to the coast of Normandy in northwestern France. It was the largest seaborne invasion force in history, and its object was to defeat Germany on its own ground. After the successful surprise landing at several points along the coast, allied forces fanned out in various directions to free France and cross the Rhine River into Germany. There they planned to meet up with Soviet forces, who had been fighting with the Allies against Germany since Hitler's treacherous attack on the Soviet Union early in the war.

The Allies reached Paris, in the center of France, by late summer, and the capital was freed on August 25. German forces withdrew across the Rhine, and the great city awoke from its long nightmare. The French people cheered and wept as the Allies marched down the broad Parisian boulevards. Flowers and paper streamers flew through the air. Haggard French soldiers, newly liberated from grim prisoner-of-war camps, some missing limbs or deeply scarred, joined the celebration. The French flag flew over the capital for the first time since 1940.

Picasso emerged from the war years with a reputation even greater than before. He was seen as a hero who had defied and outwitted the Nazis. That fall, the specially named Salon of the Liberation reserved a large hall for his recent works: seventy-four paintings and five sculptures from the war years were exhibited. Picasso's body of work now included more than 7,000 paintings, drawings, sculptures, and other pieces of artwork.

After the liberation of Paris, Picasso took a public stand on political events, which he had rarely done except in the case of the Spanish Civil War. "I don't make speeches," he once said. "I speak through painting." But in 1944 he took the controversial step of joining the Communist Party. Like his friend Eluard, he saw it as the party of the oppressed and believed that it would work against fascism and on behalf of peace. Many condemned this action, warning that the Communist leaders of the Soviet Union would soon seek to impose their system as widely as possible, beginning in Eastern Europe. This prediction would prove accurate, as the so-called Cold War followed World War II. But when Picasso took his stand, the Soviet Union was still a valued ally in the long fight against Nazi Germany.

Once Paris had been liberated, the Allied drive on Germany gained momentum. The German armies had lost countless men in their war against the Soviet Union, on what was known as the Eastern Front. Supplies, armaments, and leadership were running short as well. Although Hitler's advisors told him to avoid a two-front war by focusing his attacks on the West, he had refused to take the advice of his generals and now his forces were spread too thin. And his increasingly insane behavior had caused even loyal followers to turn against him. There had already been several failed plots against his life by his own officers. The majority of the frightened and war-weary German people were ready to surrender.

On April 30, 1945, Hitler committed suicide in his headquarters beneath the city of Berlin as British, American, and Soviet troops entered the city. A week later, Germany surrendered, and the war in Europe was over. The war in the Pacific would not end until August, after the United States had dropped the first atomic bombs on the Japanese cities of Hiroshima and Nagasaki. Several American generals had urged

President Harry Truman to take this fearful step to bring the war to an immediate end. The bomb had been developed by the secret Manhattan Project, and no one really knew what effect it would have on human beings: it had only been tested in desert areas. The horrifying results of the atomic bomb are still apparent among survivors of the firestorms and radioactive poisoning that descended upon the two cities. Japan agreed to an unconditional surrender, which was signed aboard the battleship *Missouri* in Tokyo Bay. The United States and its allies celebrated the war's end with massive parades, a hero's welcome for veterans, and laughter and tears in the streets.

In a postwar interview for the New York publication *New Masses*, Picasso explained his membership in the Communist Party. "I have always been an exile," he said. "Now I no longer am. Until the day when Spain can welcome me back, the French Communist Party has opened its arms to me, and I have found in it those that I most value."

His first postwar work, which celebrated humanity's endurance through adversity, was the lifesize bronze sculpture *Man with a Sheep*. This deeply moving work recalled both the statues of Greek shepherds of the classical age and the Christian image of the Good Shepherd, Christ, who protected his followers and laid down his life for them. One biographer observed: "In its rugged and solemn grandeur, it seems to emerge from the depth of the ages." Picasso would keep this sculpture with him for the rest of his life, through every change of residence. It was a sign of the renewed hope and vitality that would mark his work throughout the postwar period.

In her Paris home, Gertrude Stein sits beneath Picasso's portrait of her.

CHAPTER 7

A PLACE IN THE SUN

$\mathbf{F}$or many years, Picasso had spent holidays in
southeastern France on the beautiful Mediterranean
coast known as the *Côte D'Azur* (Blue Coast), also
called the Midi. Its climate and scenery were not
unlike those of his birthplace, Málaga. Along this
coast, the sea and the cloudless sky draw one outdoors
to enjoy the white beaches, the rustling date palms,
and the magical quality of the light, which has attracted many artists to the region. The warm climate
encourages the growth of thousands of flowers, and
vines climb the walls of pastel-colored villas that cling
to steep hillsides overlooking the water.

During the war years, Picasso had formed a close relationship with a gifted young painter named Françoise Gilot, who broke with her family to become his common-law wife in 1946. She was forty years younger than he. They had known each other for three years, but Françoise had maintained some distance in the relationship because she foresaw the potential problems. "Beginning in 1945," she recalled, "there were several periods when I completely stopped seeing Pablo—for a week, two weeks, or as much as two months. In spite of my feeling for him and his desire to have me with him, I had learned fairly early that there was a real conflict between our temperaments. For one thing, he was very moody: one day brilliant sunshine, the next day thunder and lightning."

When their friendship began, Picasso was hardly encouraging. When Françoise expressed the hope that she wasn't visiting his studio too often, he told her with a grin, " there are others who bore me more than you do." Through mutual friends, Françoise knew that Picasso had left his wife in 1935, that he saw little of his son, and that he visited his daughter only occasionally. He made no secret of the fact that he was not cut out for marriage and family life, with its many demands for compromise and even self-sacrifice.

One day, Françoise recalled, she and Picasso were in his studio "looking at the dust dancing in a ray of sunlight that slanted in through one of the high windows. He said to me, 'Nobody has any real importance for me. As far as I'm concerned, other people are like those little grains of dust floating in the sunlight. It takes only a push of the broom and out they go.'"

During the early years of their friendship, Françoise had the opportunity to see Picasso in all his many moods. One day he took her to see Gertrude Stein, with whom he had maintained an off-and-on friendship for forty years (he was then in his early sixties). Throughout the visit, Stein interrogated Françoise on a variety of subjects in her sharp, imperious way while Picasso kept silent. "She wanted to know," wrote Françoise, "how well I knew her work and whether I had read the American writers. Fortunately, I had read quite a few. She told me she was the spiritual mother of them all: Sherwood Anderson, Hemingway, Scott Fitzgerald. She wanted me to understand the importance of her influence, even on those who had never come to sit at her feet, like Faulkner and Steinbeck. She said that without her, there would be no modern American literature as we knew it."

Before the visit was over, Françoise was feeling the strain of carrying on the whole conversation while Picasso sat back and watched. "It was clear," said Françoise, "that he was just letting me skirt the quicksand to the best of my ability." She felt that she was back at college, taking her oral examinations. Only when they were leaving did Picasso turn his barbed wit against his old friend. "Well, Gertrude, you haven't discovered any more painters lately?"

"She apparently sensed a trap," Françoise recalled, "and said, 'What do you mean?' He said, 'Oh, no doubt about it, Gertrude, you're the grandmother of American literature, but are you sure that in the domain of painting you have had quite as good judgment for the generation that succeeded us? When there were Matisse and Picasso to be discovered, things went well. But since then, it seems to me your discoveries have been somewhat less interesting.' "

"She looked angry," said Françoise, "but made no answer."

Picasso maintained the same kind of love/hate relationship with many of his old friends. On another occasion he took Françoise to visit Georges Braque, the painter with whom he had worked so closely during the early days of Cubism. There was still a strong bond of affection between them, but it was sorely tested by Picasso's need to prove his superiority in every situation.

"When I first saw them together," wrote Françoise, "I realized that Braque was very fond of Pablo but that he didn't trust him, knowing that Pablo was capable of any ruse or wile in order to come out on top. His lowest tricks were reserved for those he liked best, and he never passed up an opportunity to play one if you gave him the chance. And if you did give him the chance, he had no respect for you."

As she got to know Braque better, Françoise realized that his manner was reserved and guarded only when he was with Picasso. With others he was quite warm and outgoing. When Braque *did* manage to get the upper hand with his old friend, his manner became much freer. Occasionally, Braque came to call on them in the Midi, although he never visited them in Paris. "He doubtless knew," said Françoise, "that the result would be—as indeed it was—that Pablo would strut around afterward saying, 'You see, Braque came to me first; he realizes I'm more important than he is.' And yet, if Braque hadn't come to us, Pablo would have fussed about it for days, saying that Braque needn't think that by staying away he would induce Pablo to make the first call."

Matters were even more complex because of Picasso's jealousy. Inevitably, he and Braque shared many friends from the old days, but Picasso was so possessive that he would become furious when he found mutual friends at Braque's studio. (Of course, he rarely called to say he was coming to visit.) When he did call, Braque made sure that no mutual friends were on the scene when Picasso arrived.

Georges Braques, shown here, was co-founder of Cubism with Picasso. Their friendship was a mixture of fierce competition and deep admiration.

One day, however, Picasso stopped in with Françoise and found Christian Zervos and two other friends at Braque's. When they got outside he said to Françoise, "You see how it is, don't you? I drop in, just by chance, to see Braque, and what do I find? My best friends. It's obvious they spend their life there. But they never come to see me." When Françoise tried to reason away his resentment, he brushed her aside and told everyone who came to visit the following day, "You know, Braque finds ways of getting all my friends away from me. I don't know what he does for them, but he must do something. The result is, I don't have any friends any more. The only people who come to see me are a bunch of imbeciles who want something from me." (Which, as Françoise pointed out, "was not very flattering to the callers to whom Pablo was unburdening himself.")

Another factor that complicated Françoise's life with Picasso was the jealousy of Olga, his former wife. She wrote him long, angry letters almost daily for more than fifteen years after they parted. When she was in the south of France, she followed Picasso and Françoise to the beach and stopped them in the street to create a scene. On one of these occasions, he slapped her. "At that," said Françoise, "she began to scream. The only way he could get her to calm down was to say, 'If you keep this up, I'm going for the police.' Then she quieted down and dropped back to a distance of three or four yards, but kept on following us wherever we went." After the birth of Françoise's son Claude in 1947, Olga's attentions became even more frequent and more hostile.

Picasso's ill will toward his former wife was often vented on their son Paulo, who was now in his early twenties. Paulo and Françoise were so close in age that they became friends, and Françoise spent a good deal of time intervening for Paulo with his angry father. One night the young man was involved in a wild party that ended with a complaint from the local police. Picasso was furious. He ordered Françoise to call his son into his room, and she went to find him.

"I'm not going in there alone," Paulo said to Françoise. "You walk in front of me."

"Since Paulo was six feet one," recalled Françoise, "I couldn't hide him entirely, even though he was crouching down behind me. Pablo began to bellow, 'You worthless creature! You carried on again last night just like the lowest form of animal existence!' He grabbed his shoes from the floor and threw them at us, then the books from his night table, and anything else he could lay his hands on. One of the books bounced off my head. I protested that I had nothing to do with this.

"'Never mind trying to pass the buck,' Pablo said. 'He's my son. You're my wife. So he's yours, too. It amounts to that, anyway. Besides, you're the one who's here. I can't go out looking for his mother. You've got to stand up and take your share of the responsibility.' Paulo and I burst out laughing at this brand of logic, but that only made Pablo angrier."

After he met Françoise, Picasso spent less and less time in Paris. He bought a series of studio-homes along the coast and traveled between them as the mood took him. His first postwar trip to the Côte D'Azur was in July 1945. He revisited the port of Antibes with Yugoslavian photographer Dora Maar and other friends. Maar had photographed the *Guernica* mural several times during its production, and she often modeled for Picasso. Photographs from the war years show several sculptures of her, and she appeared in such paintings as the 1942 *Portrait of Dora Maar*.

One of the other artists attracted to the region was Henri Matisse, who had spent much of the past thirty years in the town of Nice. Now seventy-seven years old, he was still active and still trying out new methods. He considered the Chapel of the Rosary, painted

Matisse had a profound affect on Picasso's work. He was, as Pierre Cabanne put it, "a brotherly rival."

for the Dominican nuns at Vence, his masterpiece. The colored light of its stained-glass windows still falls on the white walls of the chapel decorated with mural-size black line drawings on white tile. No longer able to walk, he made the large drawings on the walls of his room with a thick, long-handled brush and India ink.

Matisse had also begun to make painted paper cut-outs, which he called "drawing in color" with his scissors. This was the method he used to design the windows and vestments for the Dominican chapel. Picasso so admired these capelike vestments, worn by the priest to celebrate the liturgy, that he undertook the design of a bullfighter's cape in many colors. "After all is said and done," he once said, "there is only Matisse." (In fact, both men have been called "the artist of the century.") Picasso and Françoise often visited Matisse.

While Picasso was staying at Antibes, the curator of the local museum, housed in the Grimaldi Palace, offered him space in the museum for painting. At once, Picasso set to work on twenty-two large panels, painted on plywood and wallboard because canvas was still scarce. The panels included still lifes of sea creatures, studies of local villagers, and a series of light-hearted scenes from mythology, including *Satyr*, *Faun*, and *Centaur*. The largest of these compositions was the carefree *Joie de Vivre (Joy of Life)*, which celebrated the beauties of the region and its ancient ties to the classical world. "It is odd," Picasso once said, "but in Paris I never draw any fauns, centaurs or mythological heroes. It is as if they only lived here."

Other visitors to Antibes that summer included several old friends, among them the poet Paul Eluard and his wife. Eluard was a gentle, soft-spoken man, temperamentally the opposite of Picasso, and they rarely quarreled. Françoise said that "Paul was the kind of person who obtained the best from everyone."

André Breton returned from his wartime exile in the United States, but he refused to shake hands with Picasso because of his membership in the Communist

Joie de Vivre (The Joy of Life, 1946), Picasso's vision of the beauty of Antibes and the richness of the classical world.

Party. They had been friends for years, but they would not meet again. To balance this rejection, there was a warm tribute from Jaimé Sabartés: the publication of his book *Picasso: Portraits et Souvenirs*.

When Picasso's son Claude was born to Françoise in 1947, the artist began looking for a home of his own. He found it in the village of Mougins, above the scenic Bay of Cannes. Once a seaside fishing village, Cannes had gradually become a resort for wealthy British, Russian, and American travelers in search of a warm place for the winter. During the late 1940s, Cannes became the site of a major international film festival, confirming its reputation for glamor. The palm-lined Boulevard de la Croisette divided a long row of luxury hotels, fashionable shops, and art galleries from the clean sweep of the beach. But Picasso sought the seclusion of a modest house on a nearby hillside—the Villa la Galloise, which was shaded by mulberry trees.

Near the villa was the town of Vallauris, which means "Valley of Gold." It had been famous as a pottery-making center since Roman times, but the industry had fallen into a decline. Picasso became friendly with the owner of the Madura Pottery, and he began to experiment with ceramics in its workshop. After modeling an object in clay and firing it at high temperatures, one could glaze the surface and paint it with various designs. Ceramics made it possible to combine form and decoration in a great variety of ways.

Picasso had become fascinated by the owls that appeared outside his villa every evening to search for prey. When one of the birds was found injured, he took it in and cared for it. At Vallauris he made a whole series of life-size owl figures, strikingly painted and mounted on pedestals. Later, he added owls with the faces of men and women. It was his way to make endless variations on a single theme, until he had tested all the possibilities of a particular object or medium. As he explained it, "I'm always saying to myself: 'That's not right yet. You can do better.' It's rare when I can prevent myself from taking a thing up again—*x* number of times, the same thing."

Other experiments in pottery included platters in the shapes of fish, jugs with the heads and necks of animals on four-footed bases, and female figures, including *Lady in Mantilla* and *Woman on a Tile*. During his first year in Vallauris, Picasso produced about 2,000 pieces, copies of which are still sold in the village.

In 1948 Picasso traveled to Poland for the Congress of Intellectuals for Peace. There he visited the former concentration camp at Auschwitz and the Warsaw Ghetto, where thousands of Polish Jews had been massacred by the Nazis. The president of the Polish Republic awarded him a medal for his commitment to international peace. The following year he drew his famous *Dove of Peace* for the Peace Conference that was held in Paris. It appeared on all the announcements for the congress and was quickly adopted as a symbol by the international peace movement. When Picasso's second daughter was born to Françoise that spring, she was named Paloma — Spanish for "dove."

Picasso returned to Vallauris in the spring of 1949 and rented an old perfumery as a studio for painting and sculpting. The most intense period of his involvement with ceramics was over, and sculpture would be his main interest for some time. Another interest was his two young children, of whom he made several paintings in 1950, including *Claude and Paloma* and *Claude and Paloma at Play*. Although he was now in his sixties, he could still enter into a child's games and activities. Many photographs from this period show him playing with the children on the beach at Golfe-Juan, a popular resort.

The sculptures on which Picasso was working at Vallauris were mainly assemblages made from objects found in the vicinity. One of the best known of these Readymades is *She-Goat*. Its back was formed from a palm leaf, its rib cage from a wicker basket, and its udder from two ceramic flowerpots. These objects were joined with clay and the work was later cast in bronze. *She-Goat* was a familiar figure in Picasso's garden. In fact, the sculpture often had a real goat tethered to it, grazing on the grass!

At the same time, Picasso had started work on a new series of paintings inspired by works of the old masters: *Women on the Banks of the Seine*, after Courbet and *Portrait of a Painter*, after El Greco, both painted in 1950. But the harmony that had been present in his work for some years was disturbed by the course of world events. War broke out in the Asian country of Korea that same year, when Communist forces from North Korea invaded the Republic of South Korea. Then the United States and United Nations became involved militarily. Picasso's response was the painting *Massacre in Korea*, in which a group of robot-like monsters point their weapons at a group of naked women and children. As in *Guernica*, the theme was the murder of the innocent.

Massacre in Korea was extremely unpopular. No one wished to be reminded of the horrors of war so soon after World War II. Picasso was bitter about this rejection of his work, which was unusual for him. "Poor painters!" he exclaimed. "They paint the man with the machine gun, the massacring robot, the man with the repeating rifle, the man with the gun, and people tell them they cannot distinguish the uniform. They paint the massacre of the innocents, and they are told the innocents ought to look prettier than that."

The outbreak of violence in Korea was distressing to all who had hoped for a permanent peace. It moved Picasso to begin work on two major paintings, *War* and *Peace*. He decided to create a "temple of peace" in an unused fourteenth-century chapel in Vallauris. In 1952 he made the first studies for these large panels and soon filled three sketchbooks. Another example of Picasso's reaction to current events is the stark still life *Goat's Skull, Bottle, and Candle*, which recalls the works of the World War II years.

In November, Picasso was saddened by the death of his old friend Paul Eluard. He attended the funeral in Paris and returned to Vallauris to complete the two great panels for the temple of peace. "If peace prevails in the world," he said, "the war I have painted will belong to the past. Then war will be spoken of in the past tense, and all the rest will be in the present and future."

Over the next ten years, two themes alternated in Picasso's work: his own life and his fascination with the paintings of the old masters. From his personal life we have many paintings of his two younger children and their mother, pictures of his various Mediterranean studios, and sun-filled scenes of flying and nesting doves, including the birds that he kept as pets, as he had done in boyhood. As his friend Kahnweiler put it, "One must always remember that no art is more autobiographical than Picasso's. It is a perpetual confession. Such an art is more true, more sincere than any other."

Of Picasso's variations on great artists of the past, another biographer suggests that " they seemed to strengthen his own authentic personal style." Thus the two themes ran along side by side, like streams that eventually converge to form a single watercourse.

   During the early 1950s, Picasso's relationship with Françoise began to deteriorate. He started to resent the amount of time and attention that Claude and Paloma required. It was a repetition of the pattern that had begun in his first marriage when Paulo was three or four years old.

In a conversation with the poet and novelist Louis Aragon, shortly after Paloma's birth, Picasso asked, "How can you go on always loving the same woman? After all, she's going to change like everybody else and grow old." Aragon laughed at him and said, "You're an eternal adolescent, I'd say. You're not mature enough to understand."

Françoise reflected in her memoir, "At the time I went to live with Pablo, I had felt that he was a person to whom I could, and should, devote myself entirely, but from whom I should expect to receive nothing beyond what he had given the world by means of his art. I consented to make my life with him on those terms. At that time I was strong because I was alone."

But Françoise's health and energy began to flag after the birth of her second child, and she felt the need for more warmth and emotional support than Picasso was capable of providing.

> Now that the children were regulating our lives to a great extent, it began to be clear that Pablo was chafing under so much domesticity. I could almost hear him thinking,"Well, I suppose now she figures she's won the game. She's taken over, with her two children, and I'm just one of the family. It's total stabilization." And if ever a human being was not cut out for total stabilization, that was Pablo. What he himself had wanted so badly and at first had brought him such great pleasure began to rub him the wrong way. He seemed, at times, to look on the children as weapons I had forged to be used against him and he began to withdraw from me.

Gradually, Picasso began to spend more and more time away from home. He increased his demands on Françoise in that he turned over most business matters, correspondence, dealings with Kahnweiler, and other such tasks to her. But their personal relationship became increasingly distant. As Françoise faced the crisis in their relationship, she thought of the women who had preceded her in Picasso's life. "He had left each of them," she reflected, "although each of them was so wrapped up in her own situation that she thought she was the only woman who had ever really counted for him. I saw it as a historical pattern: it had never worked before; certainly it was doomed this time too. He himself had warned me that 'my love could last for only a predetermined period.' Every day I felt that ours had one less day to go."

Françoise finally decided to return to Paris with the children in the fall of 1953. When he heard her decision, Picasso was angry and bitter.

"You imagine people will be interested in *you*?" he said. "They won't ever, really, just for yourself. Even if you think people like you, it will only be a kind of curiosity they will have about a person whose life has touched mine so intimately. And you'll be left with only the taste of ashes in your mouth. If you attempt to take a step outside my reality—which has become yours, inasmuch as I found you when you were young and unformed and I burned everything around you— you're headed straight for the desert. And if you go, that's exactly what I wish for you."

After Françoise returned to Paris she never saw him again.

Old age did not diminish Picasso's creative drive.

CHAPTER 8

"NOTHING IS MORE IMPORTANT..."

In 1953 Picasso was seventy-two years old—an age at which many people have retired. On the contrary, he continued to live and work with unabated zest. "Nothing," he once said, "is more important than to create enthusiasm."

Of course, he knew that his time was limited, and he faced old age with the mixed feelings that accompany every stage of life. As he said to a friend, "I have the impression that time is speeding on past me more and more rapidly. It's the movement of painting that interests me, the dramatic movement from one effort to the next. I have less and less time, and yet I have more and more to say."

In 1953 Picasso bought another home on the Mediterranean, at Cannes. The Villa La Californie was a rambling, colorful, late-Victorian mansion with a huge natural garden. The former living and dining rooms were combined in the Great Studio, giving the artist ample space in which to pursue all his activities. Shortly thereafter, two new models appeared in his work: slender, blonde, Sylvette David and graceful, dark-haired, Jacqueline Roque. Sylvette served as the model for a monumental concrete sculpture of a woman's head installed at New York University in New York City. Picasso's best-known portrait of the woman who would soon become his third wife is *Jacqueline with Roses*, painted in 1954. In a drawing made that same year, a young Harlequin of the kind Picasso had painted long before bows to a young model from behind the mask of an older artist. It is an ironic self-portrait of the aging painter—part of a series called *The Human Comedy*.

Jacqueline's beauty inspired several paintings in the style of the old masters—riding a horse, as in a Velázquez, and looking through heavy veils, in the manner of a Goya. His new studio-home, La Californie, had a magnificent view of the sea, and Picasso painted his studio and other decorative rooms of the house repeatedly. *The Studio* of 1955 is a colorful glimpse of Picasso's workplace, strewn with paintings and sculptures in cheerful disorder. Through the elaborate windows one sees the palm trees and other foliage of the garden. A 1957 work, *Pigeons at La Californie*, shows the loft-balcony where the pigeons nested, flying freely in and out. Cannes can be seen in the distance, and beyond it the serene blue of the Golfe-Juan. Jacqueline's figure appears in many of the studio paintings.

The Picassos entertained many friends at La Californie, including Hélène and Pignon Parmelin and the photojournalist David Douglas Duncan, who published several books about Picasso. Hélène Parmelin recalled one of those visits, which led up to the 1955 drawing *Jacqueline as Lola de Valence*, after Edouard Manet. Manet's painting of the Spanish beauty in her ruffled dress and mantilla had recently arrived at the museum in Nice, and the whole party was eager to see it. "Picasso and Pignon were in the studio," Hélène remembered. "Manet was clearly the only painter in the world, and they discussed all his canvases. They talked about him for an hour. We went off, all four of us, as delighted as if we were going to see the queen. We found the Museum, full of Napoleonic relics and very pretty. We hurried up the steps. It would be splendid, Picasso said, if we saw her come to the top of the steps to receive us, as at a ball, with her mantilla and her fan. And with Manet on her arm."

In fact, Picasso's imagination at this time was almost entirely caught up in other artists and their subjects. The mythological themes he had explored during the 1930s and '40s gave way to an almost total preoccupation with interpretations of the work of other artists. In a single two-month period during the winter of 1954-55, he created more than twenty variations of Eugene Delacroix's *The Women of Algiers*.

Delacroix, born near Paris in 1798, was the foremost artist of the French Romantic school of painting. He drew much of his inspiration from literary sources, including the works of William Shakespeare, Sir Walter Scott, and medieval or Renaissance history. During a visit to North Africa in 1832, Delacroix became fascinated with the Middle East: he loved exotic subjects like the veiled, harem women and used brilliant color with great effectiveness. Picasso had studied *The Women of Algiers* closely at the Louvre and had made sketches from it as early as 1940.

Hélène Parmelin tells us that the entire household

was caught up in Picasso's day-and-night work on his versions of the Delacroix painting. One day he said, "I have a feeling that Delacroix, Giotto, Tintoretto [two great Renaissance painters], El Greco, and the rest, as well as all the modern painters, the good and the bad, are standing behind me watching me at work."

In 1957 this process was repeated in Picasso's twenty variations on the Velázquez painting *The Maids of Honor* (see Chapter 1). For this series, he moved to the second floor of the house, where no one lived but the doves, and painted obsessively throughout the fall.

Picasso's first and largest painting of the series kept the original cast of characters—the royal family and the artist painting them. (For the dog in the fore-ground, he substituted his dachshund, Lump.) The figure of the artist on the left, holding his palette, is huge in comparison to the others—much larger than life. In the smaller canvases that followed, this group

Jacqueline Roque, Picasso, and Jean Cocteau at a bullfight.

Picasso in 1966 working on the last piece of ceramic he created.

disappeared and reappeared in a bewildering variety of styles, moods, and colors.

What was Picasso doing in this series? One critic suggests that he was doing what he had once described to Françoise: "I want to draw the mind in a direction it's not used to and wake it up." In *The Maids of Honor*, says one critic, "It is as if he had taken the characters of Velázquez, kept them in that room, and put them through the trials of Alice in Wonderland. Instead of capturing the sense of mystery of the Velázquez, he gives us a series of puzzles to solve."

In 1958 Picasso bought another elegant house in the Mediterranean region of southeastern France, this one in Provence, where Cézanne had lived and worked. Picasso's purchase of the Château de Vauvenargues included most of the northern slopes of Ste. Victoire, "Cézanne's mountain" as he called it. The Château was in a remote setting not far from the city of Aix-en-Provence.

Relaxed and friendly, this is a land of red stone farmhouses with tiled roofs whose walls are wreathed in green vines. The towns of this ancient region perch on barren hills that rise suddenly from the fields. The village cafes and shady plane trees provide gathering places for old men who sip their wine or play *boules*—a form of bowling.

Provence is bounded by the marshy Camargue, famous for its birds and wild horses, and the Alpine foothills, where flowers are grown for France's perfume industry. Most of the region is dry but fertile, and the landscape and the bullfight arenas of Arles and Nimes might well have reminded Picasso of Spain. Provençales have seen many civilizations come and go: the Greeks, the Romans, the Arabs, the French monarchy. They have learned the wisdom of adapting themselves.

Cézanne left a lyrical description of this region in addition to his many paintings of its light-filled scenes:

> The air is deliciously sweet, the sun is already warming the earth, and yet the air remains sharp and dry and even tasty, like a wine. The air smells of honey, thyme, lavender, all the herbs of the nearby hills.

In Aix-en-Provence, a handsome city filled with fountains and tree-lined boulevards, one can still visit the Avenue Paul Cézanne, where the artist's small house and garden have been left as they were during his lifetime. His cape and beret still hang in the corner of his studio. Nearby, the chalky face of Mont Ste. Victoire stands out across the countryside, reflecting the various colors of the times of day and the changing seasons.

As at La Californie, Picasso painted and drew the new house—sometimes as a kind of theatrical stage setting or a rich background to his artistic activities.

The Château had a romantic quality, and the paintings of 1959 are handsome and decorative. Jacqueline, too, was painted romantically, and on one of these portraits the artist inscribed the words "Jacqueline de Vauvenargues."

Both Picasso and his wife formed a strong attachment to the house. At the same time, they missed the closeness to the sea and the many activities of the Mediterranean coast. So they also bought a rambling villa surrounded by olive trees in the village of Mougins, north of Cannes. This villa, Notre Dame de Vie (Our Lady of Life), had extensive gardens filled with olive trees, dark cypresses that bowed in the wind, and colorful flowers. Here Picasso had a studio built for himself with large windows, but he did not paint it as he had done in other houses. One biographer suggests that "Notre Dame de Vie seems to have represented a period in which Picasso had turned in on himself, on his own resources and in particular on his own life."

In the summer of 1961, Picasso made the last of his extensive variations on the work of another artist, this time Manet. He had been doing preliminary work on drawings from the painting *Déjeuner sur l'Herbe* (*Luncheon on the Grass*) for several years. These paintings of an artist and his model in an outdoor, or pastoral, setting were richly colored and decorative in their effect. They recall a comment that Picasso once made. "In reality," he said, "one works with few colors. What gives the illusion of their being many is simply the fact that they have been put in the right place." This series included a total of 27 paintings and 140 drawings.

During the last decade of his life, which he spent largely at Notre Dame de Vie, Picasso was less in the public eye than he had been for many years. He seemed to be living out a statement he had made many years before: "Nothing can be done without solitude. I have made for myself a solitude unsuspected by anyone."

In the secluded garden at Notre Dame de Vie, Picasso reviewed and redrew his life. In 1966, on his eighty-fifth birthday, the museums of Paris organized simultaneous exhibitions of his work. They included paintings, sculptures, and prints from his earliest years to his most recent work.

Two years later, the aging artist produced a series of 347 etchings on the theme of passionate love. They were published as *Suite 347*, which recalled the drawings made for the *Human Comedy* series of 1954. On the first page, Picasso appears as a spectator at the "theater" of the world he has created in his art. Plate 81 shows the artist holding a mask before his face. In Plate 111, he appears as a child crowned with laurels, the traditional sign of a victor. Other etchings included the familiar themes of the circus, the bullfight, and Spanish literature.

In 1968 Picasso's old friend Sabartés died. In his memory the artist donated his *Maids of Honor* series to the Picasso Museum in Barcelona. By now many friends were gone: Gertrude Stein, Paul Eluard, Jean Cocteau, Georges Braque. Soon there would be almost no one who remembered the early days in Paris, the struggle to establish Cubism as a style, and the theater work for the Russian Ballet. But Picasso went on working.

In 1970 Picasso's family in Barcelona donated all the paintings and sculptures in their possession to the city's Picasso Museum (one of the few museums named for an artist during his lifetime). The artist donated many of his works to the museum at the same time. That summer, his friends Christian and Yvonne Zervos held an exhibition of his recent works at the stately Palace of the Popes in Avignon, Provence.

More than 200 paintings and drawings from the previous year were shown. It was a year of retrospectives, including, in the United States, "Picasso: Master Printmaker," "The Cubist Epoch," and "Four Americans in Paris: The Collections of Gertrude Stein and Her Family" (thirty-eight of the forty-seven works were by Picasso).

The paintings of Picasso's last years have been described as "Baroque": ornate or flamboyant in style and richly ornamented. These qualities can be seen in such pictures as *The Kiss*, *The Matador*, and *Cavalier with Pipe*. The latter two recall the artist's Spanish heritage, which was so vital to his art. Picasso's own intense black eyes seem to stare from the face of the 1971 painting *Young Bather with Sand Shovel*.

To the end of his life, Picasso retained his enthusiasm, imagination, and energy. He struck a balance between his life as a public figure and the privacy he needed to pursue his vocation. Unlike most artists, he became a wealthy man, leaving an estate valued at some three hundred million dollars. But his wealth never seemed to distract him from his passion for his work.

Picasso's friend David Douglas Duncan tells us that when he died at Notre Dame de Vie on April 8, 1973, "he had worked until nearly daylight. He slept very little." He was ninety-three years old and had produced more works than any other artist who ever lived.

Picasso was buried at the Château de Vauvenargues in Provence. Over his grave, Jacqueline Picasso placed the bronze sculpture *Woman with Vase*, made at Boisgeloup in the summer of 1933. This primitive statue depicts an Earth Mother—a symbol of the constant renewal of life. There is no stone or other marking.

Picasso in his studio at Vallauris in 1954. A metal sculpture is in the foreground.

CHAPTER 9

RETROSPECTIVE

$\mathbf{H}$ow well has Picasso's reputation stood the test of time in the years since his death?

There is no sign that his reputation has diminished, although critics differ on the quality of his work from one period to another. Some believe that his work in the last thirty years of his life was not equal in quality to that of the period between 1900 and 1943. Others say that "apart from war, most of the problems of our society—mechanization, poverty, illness—have not been reflected in his painting since the Rose Period." Still others wonder why he did not produce a handful of masterpieces that took years to create, in the manner of Michelangelo or Rembrandt. They argue that his sheer productivity meant that much of his work was superficial.

In fact, it is still too soon to reach a critical consensus on his seventy-year career. But Daniel-Henry Kahnweiler, who met Picasso in 1907, said that "I was privileged to remain close to him until his death, and my admiration of his work has grown unceasingly. If I had to pick out the one quality in it that has struck me the most forcibly, I would say that it was its *freedom*." Kahnweiler explained that Picasso once confided to him, "When you start a painting you need to have an idea, but it should be a vague one."

This approach accounts for the fact that Picasso's paintings often changed completely in the creative process. Kahnweiler observed that

> he rarely made sketches with a future work in view; each picture was an end, a universe in itself. He gave his creative urge free rein, and lived only in the present. His observation "Painting makes me do what it wants" is well known. A work was finished when it seemed to him that there was nothing more to add to it. In this way one was always confronted with new solutions when one looked at his pictures. And yet these new solutions carried on the tradition, by virtue of inventing it afresh each time.

In a very real sense, it was Picasso's need to transform that made him a towering figure in the field of modern art. He had a genius for taking the best—and worst—of the past and translating it into symbols that had deep meaning for the rapidly changing present. Since he had been trained in the classical style, he could move back and forth freely between tradition and experimentation in new forms. His talent and conviction were such that others followed his lead.

Michel Leiris, a long-time friend and business associate of Picasso's, pointed out that "Picasso never believed in the barren doctrine of 'art for art's sake,' yet although he never neglected the outside world, he treated the subject of art—in the sense of the practice of art—over and over again and in many different ways." He believed the painter was an innovator, showing others how to use their eyes to see more than what is obvious at first glance. But he was also obsessed with the creative process itself and would work on a theme in many different mediums until he felt he had made it part of himself.

Perhaps another old friend of Picasso's, Henri Matisse, summed it up best in his *Notes of a Painter*. "All artists bear the imprint of their time," said Matisse, "but the great artists are those in whom this stamp is most deeply impressed."

CHRONOLOGY

1881   Picasso's birth in Málaga, Spain, on October 25.

1891   Picasso's family moves to La Coruña, Spain.

1895   The family relocates to Barcelona.

1896   Studies at La Lonja, the School of Fine Arts in Barcelona. Acquires first studio at age of fifteen.

1897   Studies at the Royal Academy in Madrid.

1898   Visits village of Horta de Ebro, in the province of Aragon, for the first time.

1899   Becomes part of the young modernist group that gathers at The Four Cats cabaret in Barcelona. Makes friends with other painters, sculptors, poets, and critics of the arts.

1900   First visit to Paris; first sales. Acquires a studio and a patron.

1901   Founds art magazine *Arte Joven* during visit to Madrid; first exhibition of his work in Barcelona.

901-04   Paris and Barcelona: Blue Period paintings. Friendship with Gertrude Stein. Settles in Montmartre section of Paris at age of twenty-two. Art dealer Ambroise Vollard mounts first exhibition of his works in France.

1905   Rose Period paintings; discovery of African art and the Post-Impressionist work of Paul Cézanne.

1907   Paints *Les Demoiselles d'Avignon,* the first Cubist work of art. Becomes friends with art dealer Daniel-Henry Kahnweiler, who offers to represent him.

1908   Painter Georges Braque forms close friendship with Picasso and begins to paint with him in the Cubist style.

1909   Early experiments in Cubist sculpture.

1912   Early works of Collage Cubism; growing reputation and influence on the worldwide art scene.

1914   *Outbreak of World War I (The Great War).* Period of solitude begins as most of Picasso's French friends enter military service. End of close collaboration with Braque.

1915   Begins to paint in the Neoclassic style as well as the Cubist; return to tradition widespread during the war years as people look to the past for security in a time of disorder and destruction.

1916   Works on scenery and costumes for the Russian Ballet production of *Parade.*

1917   Marries Russian ballerina Olga Koklova; paints her in Neoclassic style.

918-19   *World War I ends.*
Picasso and his wife continue to live in Paris and begin to spend summer vacations on the French Riviera (southeast coastal region bordering the Mediterranean).

1921   Birth of Picasso's first son, Paulo. Neoclassic painting *Three Women at the Spring* and numerous portraits of Olga and Paulo. Collage Cubist painting *Three Musicians* (two versions).

1925   Several painting styles begin to merge, as seen in the painting *The Three Dancers.* The Surrealist movement in art becomes an influence.

1926 A lifelong theme–the creative process itself–is seen in *The Painter and His Model*.

Drawing techniques become more important than ever in the works of the late 1920s and the 1930s.

1930 Myth and legend emerge as vital elements of Picasso's work. The changes of form in Ovid's *Metamorphoses* are illustrated in a series of etchings. *The Crucifixion*, a large painting on plywood, ties the theme of pain and death to the bullfight ritual.

930-35 *A severe economic depression results in poverty, unemployment, and insecurity around the world.*

The tension of the times is mirrored in Picasso's personal life and his work.

1931 Purchase of the country house at Boisgeloup; experiments in the technique of making large sculptures in metal, as taught by sculptor Julio González.

1932 New type of sculpture undertaken soon after: assemblage of found objects into three-dimensional constructions. Large retrospectives of Picasso's work held in Paris and Zurich.

932-33 Long series of paintings focus on sleeping or reclining women, with Marie-Thérèse Walter as model. The serenity of these pictures is disturbed about 1934 by symbols of danger and death, like the mythic Minotaur.

1935 *Increasing concern about the threat to world peace posed by Hitler's Nazi Germany and other aggressive nations.*

Birth of Picasso's daughter Maïa to Marie-Thérèse Walter. Combination of the bullfight and Minotaur themes in the etching *Minotauromachy*.

1936 *Outbreak of the Spanish Civil War.*
Picasso expresses his support for the Republican government of Spain, which is threatened by the revolt of conservative forces led by General Francisco Franco. Nazi Germany supports Franco.

1937 *German planes bomb the Basque town of Guernica at Franco's orders.*
The wholesale destruction of the town gives Picasso his theme for the painting commissioned by the Republican government for the Spanish Pavilion at the Paris World Exhibition. The wall-size painting *Guernica,* completed in June, shows the horror of total warfare in the massacre of men, women, and children. The painting is hailed as both a masterpiece and a warning. It is dominated by a menacing bull, which symbolizes the powers of darkness, and a dying horse, an emblem of the suffering inflicted by mindless destruction.

1939 *Outbreak of World War II; Franco triumphs in Spain.*
Painting of the large nocturne *Night Fishing at Antibes.* Major U.S. retrospective, "Picasso: Forty Years of His Art."

1940 *Occupation of France by the Germans.*
Picasso's refusal to leave Paris for safety abroad. Wartime work in the studio at 7 Rue de Augustins.

1941 *The United States enters the war against Nazi Germany and its allies, Italy and Japan.*

1942 Preliminary work for the bronze sculpture *Man with a Sheep.*

1943 *Bull's Head* assemblage.

1944 *Allied invasion of Normandy and liberation of Paris.*

Death of poet Max Jacob. Picasso retrospective at the Salon of the Liberation, showing 79 works from the war years. Progress of *Man with a Sheep*.

1945 ***World War II ends.***
Antibes revisited. Drawings for the Grimaldi Palace, now the Picasso Museum at Antibes.

1947 Birth of son Claude to Françoise Gilot and purchase of Villa La Galloise at Mougins. Intensive work in the new medium of ceramics at the Madura Pottery in Vallauris.

1948 Trip to Poland for the Congress of Intellectuals for Peace.

1949 Design for the *Dove of Peace*. Birth of daughter Paloma to Françoise.

1950 ***Outbreak of the Korean War.***
Picasso paints *Massacre in Korea*.
Numerous paintings of his children, including *Claude and Paloma at Play*. Assemblages made at the new studio in Vallauris from found objects and Readymades. New versions of works by the old masters, including El Greco.

1952 Studies for the major paintings *War* and *Peace*, designed for a temple of peace at Vallauris. Paintings completed by year's end. Still life *Goat's Skull, Bottle, and Candle*. Death of friend Paul Eluard.

1953 ***End of the Korean War.***
Purchase of the Villa La Californie, overlooking Cannes. Portraits and sculptures of Sylvette David and Jacqueline Roque. Confrontation with old age.

1954 Portrait *Jacqueline with Roses*. Series of etchings called the *Human Comedy* show an elderly artist looking on at the world he has created.

1955 Decorative portraits of the great studio at La Californie, many of them including Jacqueline.

Drawing *Jacqueline as Lola de Valence*. Variations on Delacroix's *Women of Algiers*.

1957   Variations on Velázquez's *The Maids of Honor*. Painting *Pigeons at La Californie* (several versions made during intervals of work on *Maids of Honor*).

1958   Purchase of the Château de Vauvenargues, near Aix-en-Provence. Paintings of the studio there.

1959   Portrait inscribed "Jacqueline de Vauvenargues."

1961   Purchase of another villa at Cannes, Notre Dame de Vie. Construction of a large studio there where Picasso worked in comparative seclusion. Variations on *Déjeuner sur l'Herbe*, after Manet.

1966   Simultaneous exhibitions of his work in the museums of Paris in celebration of his eighty-fifth birthday. Another painting on the theme of the painter and his model—*Painter at His Easel*.

1968   Production of 347 etchings within a six-month period, published as *Suite 347* (another treatment of the aging-artist theme taken up in the *Human Comedy* series). Death of Jaimé Sabartés. Donation of the *Maids of Honor* series to the Picasso Museum in his memory.

1970   Picasso and his family make additional donations to the Picasso Museum. Retrospective exhibitions at Avignon, France, and three major American museums. Paintings *The Matador* and *Cavalier with Pipe*.

1971   Painting *Young Bather with a Sand Shovel*. Retrospective of his works in the Grand Gallery of the Louvre on the occasion of his ninetieth birthday.

1973   April 8: Picasso's death at Notre Dame de Vie and burial at the Château de Vauvenargues.

GLOSSARY

armature   A framework used by a sculptor to support a figure being modeled in a pliable material, such as clay or plaster.

ceramic   A product made from clay or other non-metallic minerals fired at high temperature after molding.

collage   An artistic composition made of various materials, such as paper, cloth, or wood, glued onto a picture surface.

commedia dell'arte   Italian comedy of the sixteenth to eighteenth centuries, using stock characters, like Harlequin, Pantalson, and Columbine, in satirical, improvisational plots.

commission A specific work undertaken by an artist for an agreed upon payment

engrave To cut figures, letters, or devices on a surface such as metal or wood for printing.

etching An image produced by printing from a metal plate on which a picture or design has been impressed by acid.

Fauvism A movement in painting of the early twentieth century characterized by vivid colors, free treatment of form, and a vibrant and decorative effect. Henri Matisse was the most influential artist of this movement.

found objects Natural or manmade objects incorporated into or displayed as a work of art.

glaze A glossy waterproof coating applied to ceramics or other artifacts.

gouache A method of watercolor painting in which colors in cake or paste form are mixed with water and a binding substance, such as glycerine or resin.

graphic A type of image formed by drawing.

Impressionism Late-nineteenth-century movement in painting in which objects were depicted by means of dabs or strokes of unmixed colors to capture the effect of reflected light.

lithography The process of printing from a flat surface (as a smooth stone or metal plate) on which the image to be printed is ink-receptive and the blank area around it is ink-repellent. The print resulting from this process is called a lithograph.

maquette A small preliminary model of a larger work, such as a sculpture or a building.

medium The material or technical means of artistic expression. Material means include clay, paint, marble, or other substances used by the artist.

Technical means include such processes as engraving, lithography, painting, and sculpture.

mentor A trusted counselor or guide.

monochromatic Having one color or hue.

mural A painting made on a wall or ceiling surface, or a painting of wall size on a material like canvas or plywood.

palette A thin oval or rectangular board that a painter holds and on which colors are mixed.

pastel A drawing made with a paste of ground color or chalk.

portrait A pictorial or sculptural representation of a person. A sculptural portrait of head and shoulders only is called a bust.

Post-Impressionism A movement in painting that turned from late-nineteenth-century Impressionist concentration on color and light toward emphasis on volume (depth), picture structure, and other aspects of painting.

Readymade A commercial artifact selected and displayed as a work of art.

relief A type of sculpture in which forms and figures rise from the background of a flat surface or panel.

retrospective A comprehensive exhibition showing the work of an artist over a span of years.

surrealistic A work of art, including painting, sculpture, or drama, having a strange dreamlike quality.

BIBLIOGRAPHY

Barr, Alfred H., Jr. *Masters of Modern Art*, 3rd ed., rev. New York: The Museum of Modern Art, 1958.

Berger, John. *The Success and Failure of Picasso.* New York: Pantheon Books, 1965.

Blunt, Anthony, and Poebe Pool. *Picasso: The Formative Years.* London: Studio Books (Longacre Press), 1962.

Duncan, David Douglas. *Viva Picasso: A Centennial Celebration, 1881-1981.* New York: The Viking Press, 1980.

Gilot, Françoise, and Carlton Lake. *Life with Picasso.* New York: McGraw-Hill, 1964.

Hill, Ann, ed. *A Visual Dictionary of Art.* Greenwich, CT: The New York Graphic Society, 1974.

Jaffé, Hans L.C. *Pablo Picasso*. Trans. from the Dutch by Norbert Guterman. Garden City, NY: Doubleday & Co., 1980.

Janson, H.W. *History of Art: A Survey of the Major Visual Arts from the Dawn of History to the Present Day*. New York: Harry N. Abrams, 1962.

Kay, Helen. *Picasso's World of Children*. Garden City, NY: Doubleday & Co., 1965.

Lyttle, Richard B. *Pablo Picasso: The Man and Image*. New York: Atheneum, 1989.

Penrose, Roland. *Portrait of Picasso*. New York: The Museum of Modern Art, 1971.

Pontus Hulten, K.G. *The Machine: As Seen at the End of the Mechanical Age*. New York: The Museum of Modern Art, 1968.

Raboff, Ernest. *Pablo Picasso*. New York: Doubleday & Co., 1982.

Raynal, Maurice. *Picasso: Biographical and Critical Studies*. Trans. from the French by James Emmons. Geneva: Editions d'Art Albert Skira, 1953.

Read, Herbert. *A Concise History of Modern Sculpture*. Praeger World of Art Series. New York: Frederick A. Praeger, 1964.

Stein, Gertrude. *The Autobiography of Alice B. Toklas*. London: Arrow Books Ltd., 1960 ed.

Sutton, Denys, and Pablo Lecaldano. *The Complete Paintings of Picasso: Blue and Rose Periods*. Classics of the World's Great Art series. New York: Harry N. Abrams, 1968.

Venezia, Mike. *Picasso*. Getting to Know the World's Greatest Artists Series. Chicago: Childrens Press, 1988.

INDEX

A

Acrobat's Family with a Monkey, 42
Actor, The, 42
Apollinaire, Guillaume, 34, 35-36, 38, 49
Aragon, Louis, 98
Arte Joven (Young Art) magazine, 31
Arts, The, magazine, 62
Assemblages, 44, 61, 78, 79, 96
Autobiography of Alice B. Toklas, The, 48

B

Ballet, set for, 50
Barcelona, 19, 25-27, 30-31, 34, 35
Bareback Rider, The, 42
Barr, Alfred H., Jr., 70
Bateau Lavoir, 35-36, 38
Blue Period, 32-41
Boy with Dog, 42
Braque, Georges, 47, 48-49, 87-90
Breton, André, 57, 94
Bullfighter's cape, Picasso's design for, 92
Bullfighting, 11-13, 17, 30, 62
Bull's Head, 78, 79
Burial of Casagemas, The, 23
Burial of Count Orgaz, The, 23

C

Casagemas, Carlos, 26, 27
Cavalier with Pipe, 109
Centaur, 93
Ceramics, 94-95
Cézanne, Paul, 39-41, 46, 105, 106
Child with a Dove, 32

Circus Period, 41-43
Cirque Medrano, 41-42
Claude and Paloma, 95
Claude and Paloma at Play, 96
Cocteau, Jean, 51
Collage Cubism, 48-49, 56, 65
Communist Party, 82, 83
Congress of Intellectuals for Peace, 95
Courbet, Gustave, 96
Crucifixion, The, 60, 63
Cubism, 45-51, 56, 62
   Collage, 48-49, 56, 65

D

Dali, Salvador, 57
David, Sylvette, 102
Déjeuner sur l'Herbe (Luncheon on the Grass), Picasso's variations on, 107
Delacroix, Eugene, 103
Demoiselles d'Avignon, Les (The Young Women of Avignon), 45-46
Desire Trapped by the Tail (play), 78
Diaghilev, Sergei, 51
Dove of Peace, 95
Dream, The, 62
Duchamp, Marcel, 49
Duncan, David Douglas, 103, 109

E

Eluard, Paul, 80, 82, 93, 97

F

Falla, Manuel de, 53

Family Group, 37
Faun, 93
Fauves "wild beasts" group of
    artists, 39
Fitzgerald, F. Scott, 52
Fitzgerald, Zelda, 52
France, occupation by Germany, 74-
    81
Franco, Francisco, 64, 69, 71
French Resistance, 75, 80

G
Gauguin, Paul, 31
Germany, Nazi, 60, 64, 73-74. *See
    also* World War II
    occupation of France, 74-81
    special privileges offered to
        Picasso, 78-79
Gilot, Françoise (Picasso's second
    wife), 26, 36, 49, 86-91, 93, 98-99
Girl Before a Mirror, 62
Goat's Skull, Bottle, and Candle, 97
Goldwater, Robert, 48
González, Julio, 61, 80
Gouel, Eve, 48, 49-50
Goya, Francisco de, 24, 102
Greco, El, 23, 96
Guernica, 24, 79, 64-67, 70

H
Harlequin's Family, The, 42
Human Comedy, The, 102

I
Impressionist movement, 31, 39

J
Jacob, Max, 34, 35-36, 49, 80
Jacqueline as Lola de Valence, 103
Jacqueline with Roses, 102
Jaffé, Hans, 24-25, 32-33
Janson, H.W., 46, 51
Joie de Vivre (Joy of Life), 93

K
Kahnweiler, Daniel-Henry, 46-47,
    97, 112
Kiss, The, 109

Koklova, Olga (Picasso's first wife),
    51-52, 54, 55, 90
Korean War, 96-97

L
Lady in Mantilla, 95
Laurencin, Marie, 38
Leiris, Michel, 112-113
Life with Picasso, 49
Little Girl with a Hat, 32

M
Ma Jolie (My Darling), 48
Maar, Dora, 91
Madrid, 22, 31
Maïa with a Doll, 58, 63
Maids of Honor, The, Picasso's
    variations on, 104-105, 108
Maids of Honor, The, by Velázquez,
    23
Málaga (Spain), 10-11, 16-17, 21
Man Leaning on Table, 28
Man with a Sheep, 78, 83
Mañache, Pedro, 30, 31, 32
Manet, Edouard, 103, 107
Massacre in Korea, 96-97
Matador, The, 109
Maternités, 54
Matisse, Henri, 39, 41, 91-92, 113
Meninas, Las (The Maids of Honor), 23
Metamorphoses, The, Picasso etchings
    illustrating, 60
Minotauromachy, 62
Mont-Sainte-Victoire, 39, 105-107
Museum of Modern Art, 70
Myth, 56, 60, 93

N
Natural History, Picasso watercolors
    illustrating, 80
New Masses, 83
Night Fishing at Antibes, 69-70

O
Olivier, Fernande, 38, 41, 47-48
Owl figures, 94-95

P

Page, Russell, 29-30
Painter and His Model, The, 60
Pallarés, Mañuel, 24
Parade (ballet), 51, 52
Paris, France, 27, 29-30, 35
Parmelin, Hélène, 102, 103-104
Parmelin, Pignon, 102
Peace, 97
Pel y Ploma (Fur and Feather), 27
Penrose, Roland, 61
Picasso, Claude (Picasso's son), 90, 94, 98
Picasso, "Maïa" Maria de la Concepción (Picasso's daughter), 58-62-63
Picasso, Pablo
  in art school, 21-22, 24
  ballet costumes and sets, 51-54
  Barcelona one-man show, 34
  birth, 7, 13
  Blue Period, 32-41
  bullfighter's cape, 92
  ceramics, 94-95
  childhood, 14-19
  Communist Party, membership in, 82, 83
  death, 109
  early influences, 23-24, 31-32
  first commission, 42-43
  first sale, 30
  love of animals, 38
  name, 8, 13-14
  Nazis, special privileges offered by, 78-79
  New Caledonia influence, 40
  paintings inspired by works of other artists, 96, 97-98, 102, 103, 104-105, 107
  Paris shows, 31-32, 35
  patron, 30, 31, 32
  personal relationships
    with Fernande Olivier, 38, 41, 47-48
    with Françoise Gilot (second wife), 86-92, 98-99
    with Jacqueline Roque (third wife), 102, 107
    with Marie-Thérèse Walter, 62-63
    with Olga Koklova (first wife), 51-52, 54, 61
  with people, 15, 88-90
  play *(Desire Trapped by the Tail)*, 78
  political beliefs, 81-82
  in poverty, 32-41
  Prado, director of, 64
  realistic painting, return to, during World War I, 50-51
  reputation since his death, 111-113
  retrospective exhibitions, 62, 70, 108, 109
  Rose (Circus) Period, 41-43
  schooling, 17, 18-19
  women, attitude toward, 36
Picasso, Paloma (Picasso's daughter), 95, 98
Picasso, Paul (Picasso's son), 54-56, 90-91
Picasso Lopez, Maria (Picasso's mother), 10, 22, 52, 70
Picasso Museum, Paris, 54
Picasso Museum of Antibes, 70
Picasso Museum in Barcelona, 108
Picasso: Portraits et Souvenirs, 94
Pigeons at La Califonie, 102
Portrait of Allan Stein, 43
Portrait of the Artist's Mother, 20, 22
Portrait of Dora Maar, 91
Portrait of Gertrude Stein, 43, 89
Portrait of Olga Koklova, 55
Portrait of a Painter, 96
Post-impressionism, 39
Prado, 22-24, 64

R

"Readymades," 49. *See also* Assemblages
Rome, Italy, 54
Roque, Jacqueline (Picasso's third wife), 102, 107, 109
Rose Period, 41-43
Rosenberg, Paul, 52
Rouault, Georges, 39
Ruiz Blasco, Don José (Picasso's father), 8-10, 14, 15, 18, 21
Ruiz Picasso, Concepción (Picasso's sister), 18
Ruiz Picasso, Lola (Picasso's sister), 17, 22

S

Sabartés, Jaimé, 17, 26, 34-35, 36, 80, 94, 108
Sala Pares, 34
Satyr, 93
Science and Charity, 22
Sculptures, 44, 47, 61, 78, 79, 95-96
Seated Woman in Blue, 76-78
She-Goat, 96
Soler, Francisco, 31, 34
Spanish Civil War, 63-64, 70-71
Spinners, The, 23
Stein, Gertrude, 13, 38, 42-43, 48, 52, 86-87
Stein, Leo, 42-43, 46
Still Life with Bull's Head, 78
Still Life with Chair Caning, 48
Studio, The, 102
Suite, 347, 108
Surrealism, 57, 78
Surrender of Breda, The, 23

T

"Temple of peace," 97
Third of May, The, 24
Three-Cornered Hat, The, 53-54
Three Dancers, The, 57, 59
Three Musicians, 42, 56
Three Women at the Spring, 54
Toulouse-Lautrec, Henri de, 31-32

U

Utrillo, Miguel, 27, 34

V

Van Dongen, Kees, 38
Van Gogh, Vincent, 31
Velázquez, Diego, 23, 102, 104-105
Violin, 44
Vollard, Ambroise, 31, 43, 71

W

Walter, Marie-Thérèse, 61-63
War, 97
Weeping Woman, 69, 72
Weill, Berthe, 30
Woman Asleep in a Red Armchair, 62
Woman on the Banks of the Seine, 96
Woman with a Cignon, 32
Woman Dressing Her Hair, 69
Woman with a Mandolin, 56
Woman on a Tile, 95
Woman with Vase, 109
Women of Algiers, The, Picasso's variations on, 103
World War I, 49-50, 65-69
World War II, 73-83
    beginnings, 60-61, 69-70

Y

Young Bather with Sand Shovel, 109
Young Boy Leading a Horse, 42
Young Girl with a Basket of Flowers, 42

Z

Zervos, Christian, 80, 108-109
Zervos, Yvonne, 108-109

Photo Credits: